CARL GORMAN'S WORLD

Carl Gorman's World

Carl on his favorite horse "March," Chinle, Arizona, 1917.

Henry and Georgia Greenberg

University of New Mexico Press • Albuquerque

Carl at U.C. Davis before Picnic Day Parade, 1971.

Library of Congress Cataloging in Publication Data

Greenberg, Henry, 1921–
Carl Gorman's world.

Bibliography: p.
1. Gorman, Carl Nelson, 1907– . 2. Navajo Indians—Biography.
I. Greenberg, Georgia, 1919– . II. Title.
E99.N3G844 1984   973'.0497   83-26072
ISBN 0-8263-0738-8

International Standard Book Number 0-8263-0738-8.
Library of Congress Catalog Card Number 83-26072.
First Edition

For Mary

Mary has been my biggest inspiration and supporter.
She is my best critic.

Carl Gorman

She graciously shared with us her extensive research, her knowledge
and understanding, her rare insight, the depths of her feeling.

Henry and Georgia Greenberg

ONE

(A PROLOGUE)

On a warm September night in 1978, in downtown San Francisco, a gallery at the corner of Mason and Sutter was holding a reception for Navajo artist R. C. Gorman. The occasion was the opening of a retrospective showing of Gorman's work. A crowd of onlookers was gathered outside on the sidewalk, attracted by the sight and sounds of the festivities inside. A security guard at the door kept out all but the privileged.

From the moment the gallery opened, it was crowded with people— a select group drawn from the preferred list of gallery clients. Dowagers and white-haired gentlemen, elegantly dressed; younger men and women, casually garbed; a cosmopolitan group, champagne glasses in hand, milled from one work of art to the next in the brightly lit spaces of the comfortable gallery rooms. The hubbub of talk and laughter was lit from time to time by flashbulbs.

Moving graciously through the crowd, seeming to enjoy every moment of it, was the vibrant figure of R. C. Gorman; his compact body clothed in a beige gabardine suit, white shirt, and dark tie; his black hair dropping down to his shoulders, held in place over the high forehead by a wide, flowered headband. He laughed easily and often.

Commanding attention was a new sculpture, the highlight of the opening. Occupying a pedestal in the center of the main gallery space, it was a bronze head, larger-than-life size, strong, proud, and powerful, entitled *Portrait of a Navajo Code Talker*. This was a portrait of the artist's father.

As all the people at the reception had known in advance, this was R. C. Gorman's tribute to his father, himself an artist of repute. It was

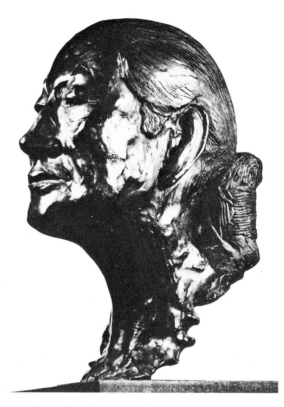

Bronze bust of Carl, entitled "Navajo Code Talker," 1978.

a tribute as well to those Navajos who, like his father, had served so brilliantly in World War II, had developed the Navajo "talking code" and used it successfully in the South Pacific invasions, a special code, within the Navajo language, that the Japanese could never break.

Standing close by the bronze head of himself was Carl Nelson Gorman, seventy years old, his six-foot body poised and straight, his tanned face handsome and unwrinkled, his graying hair bound back in the knot of white wool. He was dressed in a dark suit, a white shirt, a string of turquoise around his neck. Turquoise bracelets encased his wrists. He accepted with easy dignity the flattery of the people who gathered around him, old and young. They would not let him leave the spot. They insisted upon comparing him to the replica, the original to the model, and, splendid as the bronze portrait was, their compliments were invariably in favor of him. An elderly, bejeweled lady came through the crowded circle to shake his hand affectionately, and he thanked her with a kiss. A beautiful Indian woman approached Carl Gorman enthusiastically to embrace him, chatting about the last time they had met. Then she bent over and kissed the tip of the nose of the bronze head. She burst out with laughter at her gesture, and Carl Gorman joined in, embracing her.

2

R. C. Gorman working on bust of his father, San Francisco, 1978.

This was a happy occasion for Mary Gorman, a spirited woman in her early fifties, tall, blonde, neatly dressed in a white blouse and blue knit-jersey skirt, a coral necklace framing her oval face. She was Anglo, Carl's second wife. They had met after World War II when he returned from the South Pacific and his long service as a Marine. Mary had fallen instantly in love with him. She returned to the reservation with Carl many years later, when he came back to his own land to work among his people. She accepted his culture and religion, his way of life, and the attendant joys and the hardships. In the things of everyday existence, many thought she was more Navajo than he.

This night, in the crowded gallery, Mary watched her husband with pride. The strength of the traditional Navajo was in Carl Gorman's face, and the integrity of a man who is certain of himself, proud of his person, his identity, his culture. He was at peace and at ease anywhere. Since his youth he had moved easily in both Anglo and Navajo worlds, and he had given of himself freely in both. He kept his bond with the past, but he was receptive to the best from the present. The life of this man, an artist, a Marine, a lover of music and dance, a philosopher and teacher, touched everyone around him.

TWO

It was a bleak winter night in late December of 1915 in a remote corner of northern Arizona. Cold winds buffeted a small adobe trading post and the long, narrow home attached, standing near the mouth of Canyon de Chelly in the small community of Chinle.

Over the shrill wind, the high sounds of opera singing emerged from the home. Inside the main room, a sturdy Navajo boy of eight, Carl Nelson Gorman, was sitting cross-legged before a crude table on which an old Victrola was set, its great wide horn extending upward, the black-and-white dog on its front looking up at "his master's voice." The voice of the great Caruso soared over the room with the strains of "Celeste Aida," then slowly began to wheeze down as the record slowed to a stop. The boy leaped to his feet to wind the crank vigorously at the side of the machine. The music rose again and he dropped back to rest on the floor. He picked up the heavy stub pencil and the brown paper he had dropped and began to draw again. The long sweeping lines of one galloping horse after another covered the paper. Near him, by the light of a kerosene lamp, Carl's older sister Mary, a round-faced, chubby girl of eleven, sat reading to her six-year-old brother, Wallace. On the worn brown davenport against the wall, a month-old baby brother, Stephen, lay completely encased within the framework of a traditional cradle-board, a round hoop overhead protecting his head, which barely emerged from the buckskin laced tightly about his body.

A large, pot-bellied stove occupied the center of this living room. Just beyond, a slim Navajo woman was working at her modest-sized loom. She was the children's mother, Alice P. Gorman. Her brown hair was pulled up on top of her head in a bun. She wore a neat gingham dress, with a trim white collar. She looked up from her weaving from time to time, listening to the music. When the record finished, she asked Carl to put it on again. "Something so beautiful, Carl," she said to him, speaking English, "should be played again and again." She spoke to him as a mother and also as a teacher.

It was a lucky day, she thought, when the old Anglo came by last summer with the Victrola and a pack of heavy records on his wagon. He was tired of lugging them around, he said, trying to sell them. He knew she liked music, and he'd give the whole lot to her in trade for one of her rugs.

Now the long nights were filled with the great voices from the Golden Age of Opera, with Caruso and Galli-Curci, Melba and Scotti; and from the old solid records with the thick needle grooves on only one side would come the magnificent arias from *La Traviata* and *Il Trovatore*, from *Carmen* and *I Pagliacci*, the Quartet from *Rigoletto*, the Sextet from *Lucia*. Carl would listen, absorbing, beating his feet in rhythm. The music poured into the boy's inner being while he was drawing, continually drawing on pieces of paper, any paper he could scrounge from his father's trading post—brown bags, cardboard, scraps, anything—and always he drew pictures of horses.

In later years, Carl Gorman would never forget that scene, repeated often in his childhood home: himself as a young boy, sitting at night in the company of his mother while she wove at her loom and he drew pictures of horses. He would hear again the two of them exulting over the Grand Opera records, the great singers, the lilting, soaring music that came out of the huge Victrola horn while outside, on a winter night, the winds whistled and the snow was flying.

By this time in young Carl's life his father was already successful in business. In addition to his trading post at Chinle, he had opened a new one at Black Mountain, and he owned a large ranch with over a thousand head of cattle and many horses. "It was the horses I loved," Carl Gorman always said. As far back as he could remember, virtually as soon as he could walk, he was riding a horse. He would draw them the way he saw them, with excitement, from a child's clear, vivid impressions.

One day, Carl's father became upset with the boy's seeming obsession with "this drawing business." He berated Carl for being "damn lazy," and told his wife sternly she ought to give the boy more work to do; keep him busy with a man's work instead of just letting him sit around drawing pictures of horses all the time! But the mother defended Carl. She said he was still only eight years old and had a right to draw horses if he wanted to. Her husband had fifteen cowboys working for him, she said, and they could do the heavy work for him. Carl overheard the

Alice Gorman on horse-
back, Chinle, ca. 1912.

argument. He never forgot it. "I think if it weren't for my mother," he
said later, "I would never have become an artist."

Carl Gorman's mother, Alice Peshlakai, was born in 1885 in the
area of Crystal, New Mexico, a region of the Navajo land where the
fields were fertile and green, the hills studded with ponderosa, piñon,
and oak. The high Chuska Mountains with their towering peaks loomed
in the distance. Alice's home was a rude, two-room log house, with
hand-hewn wooden bed and furniture, the hard-packed dirt floor covered
with a carpet.

Water was plentiful for the people and for their herds of cattle and
flocks of sheep and goats. In the winter, the family was often snowed
in for weeks at a time. They were stocked with provisions to carry them
through—flour and mutton, dried fruit, coffee, corn meal, and the daily
fresh milk from their goats.

Alice was one of nineteen children born to the eminent Navajo
leader known as Peshlakai. Among the Navajos, it was an accepted
custom that a man could have several wives, and usually they were
related. Peshlakai had three wives, all sisters. Alice's mother was wife
number two; her name was Bil-ki jiz-bah; she and her sisters were of
the prominent Dibé-thlizhiní (black sheep) clan. Each of the three had
her own house and her own rights to land and grazing in widely separated, but contingent sections of the Crystal region. This meant that
Peshlakai's "domain" extended for dozens of square miles, that his children and theirs, in turn, would hold the rights to a large expanse of
valuable property for a long time to come.

His native name was Beshthlagai-ilth'ini Althts'osigi, of the Táchii'nii clan. Among the earliest of the Navajo silversmiths, he was recognized as one of the best. In the same group was Atsidi Sani, a clan
brother of Peshlakai's, who is considered by some as the first Navajo

silversmith. Carl's grandfather was known in English as "Slender maker of silver," and demand for his silver pieces was widespread in the years around 1900. At that time, he had as many as ten Navajo assistants working for him in Crystal, melting and pouring silver, and pounding out Mexican silver coins, all crowded into the long stone barn that he had converted into a factory. In addition to the silver bead or squash blossom necklaces, bracelets, rings, concho belts, Peshlakai was called upon to make more difficult objects than most other silversmiths attempted: ornate canteens, complete bridles, intricate unconventional necklaces—all of silver, with no turquoise used.

Peshlakai was among the more progressive of the Navajo leaders, and soon became a spokesman for his people. On several occasions, he went to Washington and represented the Navajo Tribe before the United States government. He had learned English well, and in a direct, laconic way he told off the Bureau of Indian Affairs officials for their continuous failures to help his people. He denounced them for the miserable treatment they imposed upon the Navajo children in their government boarding schools.

In 1893, Peshlakai went to the Chicago World's Fair, set up a booth, and displayed and sold some of his most original work there. Accompanying him to Chicago were two of the Navajo Tribe's leaders, his brother-in-law Charley Mitchell and the eminent Chee Dodge, who would one day be the first elected chairman of the Navajo government. Peshlakai returned from the World's Fair with a new respect for the white man's education and with a different viewpoint about the people with whom his people would have to deal in the future. "We have to have education to deal with these people," he said publicly. "They're not going to go away." The crux of his attitude was that education had to become vitally important to the Navajos. He began to work with the priests at the Mission of St. Michael when they planned to open a school. Many Navajos had resented sending their children off to government schools. Often the children became sick and died. Peshlakai gave permission to the head of St. Michael's to take any of his nineteen children for school, and encouraged other Navajos to do the same. Later he helped open up the teaching of Catholicism at the Fort Defiance government school. He saw no conflict in the teaching of Catholicism with the traditional Navajo religion and culture, as long as the children were being educated.

When Alice's father decided it was time for her to begin formal education, the mission school at St. Michael's had not yet opened. She started at the government school at Fort Defiance, but Peshlakai was dissatisfied with the conditions there. He sent his daughter to a different government school at Grand Junction, Colorado. Here she excelled as a student, learning to read, write, and speak English fluently. She fell in love with music, a love that would remain with her the rest of her life.

Peshlakai and Bilkijizbah, Carl's grandparents, Gallup, New Mexico, ca. 1905.

Peshlakai, ca. 1914.

Alice Peshlakai was a mature, tall, slender young woman when she returned to the reservation. She was proud of her English. She wore "American" clothes. She went to work in Fort Defiance at a small Episcopal church that had just been built. There Nelson Gorman met her and fell in love.

Nelson C. Gorman was born in 1874 near Chinle. As soon as he was old enough to go to school he was brought down to the army station at Fort Defiance. Children were gathered here to be sent off to various government schools for their education, many of them far from the reservation. The army sergeants in charge were dismayed by the long Navajo names of the children—much too hard to pronounce, they thought. For each child they selected an Anglo name from their army roster, put it on a tag, and hung it around the child's neck. That explains many of the Navajo names of today, such as McCabe, Foster, Miles, Burnside, Washington, Norcross, and Thompson.

When Carl's father got in line, his tag read *Nelson Carl Gorman*. A friend of his from Chinle was given the name John Gorman, the next on the list. Over the years, many of both John's and Nelson's blood and clan relatives took the name of Gorman, a fact that has created considerable confusion outside the Chinle area. Howard Gorman, a prominent Navajo, calls Carl his nephew, but the relationship is not what the term implies in English. They are related by clan.

At Fort Defiance, Nelson Gorman was given a neat uniform and dispatched to the Indian school at Santa Fe. He was an apt student, learned his English well, and was excellent at arithmetic and reading. He rode a horse with great skill; he was an excellent cyclist and won many races. He came back to Fort Defiance a young man, tall, lean, strong-looking, and went to work for the government there, first as a laborer, later as an interpreter.

The superintendent at Fort Defiance liked Nelson Gorman. When orders came through for him to cut government expenses and drop the Navajo interpreters, he came to Nelson to talk to him about his future. "You're a bright young man," he said. "You've got a lot of know-how. I'm going to urge you to do what very few of you Navajos have done— and that's go into business for yourself." He knew that Nelson had been saving his money. A wealthy Eastern woman had contacted the superintendent from Santa Fe and was interested in helping "worthy" Navajos to become economically independent. Her name was Doubleday. There was no doubt about the money being available. Her family owned a big publishing house in New York. With the help of the superintendent the deal was soon arranged. Nelson Gorman would open a trading post of his own. In 1903 he persuaded Alice Peshlakai to become his wife. They loaded their few possessions onto Nelson's wagon and drove twenty-five miles into the tall pine forest of Ganado Ridge to Old Sawmill.

There Nelson Gorman set up his first trading post, a small store with living quarters in the rear. Within a few months, realizing that the business possibilities at Old Sawmill were limited, he decided to give up the store. Much land in the Chinle area was controlled by his father-in-law's clan, the Táchii'nii. Nelson and Alice moved to a place on the Nazlini road eight miles southeast of Chinle, where her family had given them land. Here he built his second trading post, a rectangular structure made of local stone held firm in adobe mortar. This is where Carl Gorman was born, and the sturdy structure still stands today. Here the family lived for several years. Nelson needed water for his growing herd of cattle. With the help of his Navajo neighbors, he built an earthen dam almost a quarter of a mile long that held in the flowing creek. After a year or so, the livestock broke through the crude barrier. Nelson decided not to fix it; he had other plans.

Young Nelson Gorman, student at Santa Fe Indian School, New Mexico, ca. 1894.

House where Carl was born 1907, Nazlini Road, Chinle, as it looks today. Photo by Georgia Greenberg.

Nelson Gorman's Store Chinle Ariz.

Nelson Gorman's store at Chinle, ca. 1914.

At that time, in 1910, the U.S. government was building a school in Chinle. Nelson could see the possibility of good business with all the workers there, and he moved his family into the town. In a clearing near the Chinle Wash, he built his new trading post of stone and wood with an earthen roof. Only a few hundred yards away was the entrance to the beautiful Canyon de Chelly. The place of business was wisely chosen. It quickly began to prosper.

12

Fred Peshlakai, Rose Peshlakai, and Alice P. Gorman holding little Stephen, ca. 1915.

The Gorman family home near Chinle.

Nelson Gorman, successful trader, Chinle, ca. 1915.

Behind the trading post, the Gorman home was attached: living room, kitchen, bedroom. Later, as the children came, they would add one bedroom and then another. Soon Nelson had two barns, a mark of success. One was for the hay that he sold in large quantities; the other barn was for his horses. He had a small separate house built of stone, where a Navajo man lived and baked the store's bread, enough to be sold for an entire week, at five cents a loaf.

Nelson Gorman's trading post, like most of the others on the reservation, was more than a place to buy food, get supplies, or pick up the occasional piece of mail. It was a place of congregation for the Navajos, a social center where they could get community gossip, the latest news from Washington, D.C., and the word about missionary activities. People came from many miles away, often from hogans deep in isolated country. They would gather in the winter about the huge pot-bellied stove in the center, laugh and talk, or sit quietly for hours. The walls were lined with shelves of trade goods, canned food, articles of clothing, colorful bolts of calico, gingham, and velveteen. Hanging from the rafters were coffee pots, saddles, horse collars, and harnesses. Against the wall lay concho belts of silver, some old, some new. In a corner was a pile of Navajo rugs, brought in by the weavers of the area, to be taken to the wholesale dealers in Gallup and traded for merchandise for Gorman's store. In the adjacent storage room one could find large baskets of onions and beans, sacks of flour, salt, and sugar, sacks of wool, and a tall pile of sheepskins. In the safe, under the counter, pawn was kept—the pieces of ornamental silver that people traded for goods, which were to be held until redeemed. On top of the counter was a bulky coffee grinder with boxes of Arbuckle coffee beside it.

Nelson Gorman was ambitious and hard working. He acquired large herds of cattle that roamed from Chinle back to Black Mountain, the long ridge called today Black Mesa, known for its huge stores of coal and great open pit mines. There Nelson Gorman set up another trading post in 1912. But after two years he sold it to Lorenzo Hubbell, the well-known southwestern trader. He may have felt he was expanding too far, for he discovered how difficult it was to bring groceries and goods long distances over muddy roads. Or it may be that Hubbell made him an offer he couldn't resist—not only a generous supply of trading goods, but also a pair of handsome oversize draft horses, which Nelson Gorman could use on his farm. They were powerful, tireless, and invaluable. As a boy of eight, Carl Gorman got on their backs and rode them. He had no fear of the huge animals, and was always amazed at how much they ate. All through his life, Carl spoke about the horses of his childhood. There was beautiful, gentle Buckskin; and a white horse named March given to him for his birthday; and another called Diamond, a cattle horse, part Arabian, that every once in a while, Carl said, appeared in his dreams.

In 1915, Nelson Gorman bought an old battered Model T Ford, one of the first on the Navajo reservation. Patched up with barbed wire much of the time, the car proved to be more valuable for occasional pleasure forays into the countryside than for practical purposes. For major transportation, he used a large wagon pulled by four horses. One of his teamsters would take it to Gallup, a hundred miles away, to pick

Trading post money, Nelson Gorman's store, ca. 1917. Photo by Georgia Greenberg.

15

up supplies. The trip took three days, then three days back to Chinle, the wagon piled high with sacks of corn and hay purchased en route to feed the horses; also purchased were flour and sugar, jeans and shirts, bolts of cloth, saddles, the whole gamut of trading post goods. Carl remembered making the trip to town once with his father, going into a drugstore where the stools were very high and all the men wore pistols. Gallup was a rough cow town and railroad town in those days, he said.

For the Gorman family, the years around 1910 were a period of struggle, of progress, of accomplishment. The strength and spirit of her father, the indomitable Peshlakai, were in Alice Gorman. She worked with her husband in the trading post, trying to bring some order to the mass of merchandise, the general clutter so typical of trading posts. She was proud of Nelson's reputation as a fair dealer; he was one of the very few Navajo traders on the reservation.

In these years, too, she raised her family of six children, three boys and three girls. One girl died as a baby, one as a young school girl, and the other in her late teens. Alice always had a servant to help her take care of the children and do the housework, a Navajo woman who lived in a small bedroom of her own at the far end of the house. Chinle was cold in the winter and hot in the summer. A huge wood stove for heat and for cooking filled the back end of the kitchen. At one corner a large pantry was stocked with food. Because there was no refrigeration, keeping food cool and fresh in the intense heat of the Chinle summer was a persistent problem. Alice was determined to have some kind of cooler. She had one of the men dig deep into the ground below the pantry, and she stored her food there. But her project failed when a heavy August thunderstorm flooded the cooler, washing out all the food she had stored.

Determined to have her refrigerator, Alice Gorman asked her husband to build an extension outward from the kitchen window under the outside porch roof. She covered it with a screen and a large, thick gunnysack. From a small tank above, water dripped down slowly, steadily, like an evaporative cooler, to provide the precious refrigeration. It worked. She could now keep fresh meat and milk and the goat's-milk cheese that she made for her family and for the men who worked on the ranch.

At round-up time, there were as many as twenty Navajo cowhands. With the help of her servant, Alice prepared the daily noon meal—mutton stew, canned fruit, and stacks of flour tortillas, like the Spanish but much thicker, called "náneeskaadí."

In her father's home, Alice Gorman had been brought up in the traditional Navajo religion, following the path of the Blessingway. At the same time, she had been taught by her father that education was of paramount importance. When she went to the government school, she was also forced to go to church. Religion was a big part of the total program, as important as the three R's. Alice chose to become an Epis-

Alice Gorman, Carl seated, sister Mary standing. Photo by J. R. Willis, Gallup, New Mexico, 1909.

copalian. But she saw in this no conflict with the Navajo way.

In Chinle, there was no Episcopal church. The Episcopal priest at Fort Defiance assured Alice that under the circumstances it would be all right for her to attend the Catholic church, and send her children to its Sunday school. But Alice soon became disenchanted with this form of Christianity, with the attitude of some of the clergy in the community. She apparently still considered herself Protestant. She had contacts with the Presbyterians having sent her brothers, Fred and Paul, to the early Presbyterian mission school at Leupp, which was later moved to Ganado where it flourished. The Presbyterians had established missions in Chinle probably with Alice's cooperation.

As the years went on, Alice became very religious. With Nelson she actively went about establishing a congregation. Because there was no money to build the church at first, the people met in her home, in hogans, and at the trading post. In 1923, with the Reverend A. K. Locker, Alice spearheaded a movement to build a church on the land close to where the Gormans had their trading post.

Alice translated over thirty hymns into Navajo, old hymns like "Jesus Paid It All," "Come Through Almighty King," "Only Trust Him," and "Coming Home." It was not easy to translate the English words precisely into Navajo, since so many words have different shades of meaning in the two languages. She encouraged the women of Chinle to sing these hymns in the church choir. On Sundays they would come to her home and practice. Alice often sang the hymns in Navajo while she worked at home, in the kitchen and when she was weaving. She had a soft, lovely voice, and she kept seeking the word that would go best with the music.

Carl and the older children were away at school during most of this time and were not greatly influenced by the Presbyterian church, most especially Carl. Alice had given the children English names, spoke English with them at home, and helped them in their early years when they went to the Chinle day school to learn to read and write. From the first, Alice's home had always been oriented to the Christian, Anglo world.

With all the demands of her busy life, Alice always found time to work at her loom. For the Navajos, weaving is a part of the whole life cycle. The weaver at her loom has to weave as her life permits, sometimes more, sometimes less. For most of the women, weaving was an economic necessity. They didn't think of it as an art form.

The Navajo loom was a component of the Navajo way. Vertical, very simply built, lightweight, the loom could be moved easily. It was similar to the loom used by the Pueblo Indians. When the Navajos moved their flocks from summer range to winter range, they didn't necessarily take their loom with them. Most kept one at the summer camp and another at their winter camp.

For the Navajo people, the loom was symbolically tied to the elements of the land and to the Navajo religion and myths. Deep within Canyon de Chelly there is a monumental tower called Spider Rock. A double-turreted natural obelisk of sandstone, it rises sheer and stark more than eight hundred feet upward from the canyon floor. In the Navajo legends, told from one generation to the next, this rock tower was spoken of as the home of Spider Woman. It was she who learned the art of weaving from the web of the spider, and, according to legend, she taught this art to Navajo women. It is Spider Woman, they say, whose spirit fills the individual weaver, even today, and who helps direct their weaving.

For generations Navajo women have been known for their weaving. As early as the late eighteenth century, their work was respected. "They work their wool with more delicacy than the Spanish," said Governor Fernando de Chacón in 1795, speaking of the Navajos. By the middle of the nineteenth century the skill of the Navajo weavers was increasingly recognized. Their blankets were traded in places as far away as Mexico, or at posts in Taos, Santa Fe, and Bent's Fort. The wools used were primarily in their natural state, creamy whites, browns, and blacks. By carding two colors together, colors could be varied among grays, tans, and other shades of brown.

By the 1850s, weavers were beginning to use imported red yarns and indigo for blue dye, introduced to them by the traders. With the German invention of aniline dye in 1856, a wide range of bright colors—red, orange, green, purple, yellow—became available. These dyes soon were distributed throughout the world. Within a decade, they were brought into the American Southwest, and by 1880, the aniline dyes, inexpensive and easy to work with, were in common use among Navajo weavers. Also, the four-ply, aniline-dyed yarn called Germantown, after the Pennsylvania town where it was manufactured, came into use. The women took delight in the color intensity of the new dyes, and they began to experiment in bright new designs for their blankets which became popularly known as "eyedazzlers." Many were garish. But many showed creativity and imagination.

Before 1890, the coming of the railroad through the Southwest had a great effect on the state of Navajo weaving. Trading posts were set up along the route of the trains. In the next two decades, the white traders brought in and sold the inexpensive machine-made Pendleton blankets which the Navajos began to use. They also encouraged the women to make rugs instead of blankets, for these would be a more marketable product. During this period, the quality of Navajo weaving declined considerably, with the emphasis on quantity. Aniline dyes and coarser yarns were used heavily, and many traders had a policy of paying for rugs by weight instead of quality of design.

Yet at this very same time, there were some traders whose concern for a fine commercial product actually saved the craft, among them, J. B. Moore of Crystal, Lorenzo Hubbell at Ganado, and C. N. Cotten, who left his association with Hubbell and opened a wholesale house in Gallup. They paid bonuses for craft quality, set high standards for design, and encouraged the women to be more restrained in their use of color. Moore suggested to his weavers that they use borders on their rugs with oriental motifs and patterns. These designs were reminiscent of the oriental rugs familiar to buyers from the East.

Hubbell encouraged the weavers who came to him to go back a generation to the classic patterns of the mid-nineteenth century using black, white, red, and blue. He hung reproductions of these old patterns on the walls of his trading post in Ganado for the weavers to see and reproduce.

C. N. Cotten was among the first to merchandise the weavers' work through advertising leaflets and eventually illustrated catalogues. This made it possible for people in different parts of the country to order rugs according to the pattern and the weave they preferred.

Alice Gorman's mother was a weaver in Crystal during the latter part of the nineteenth century. From the day that Alice could hold strands of wool, she began to weave at her own small loom, watching and imitating her mother. Alice's sister Mary became an outstanding weaver, and later taught at the Albuquerque Indian School. Their niece, Katherine, taught weaving there too, and then went on to the Fort Wingate and Fort Lewis Indian schools, achieving a reputation as a distinguished weaver.

As a small boy in Chinle, Carl Gorman was always intrigued by his mother's weaving. Watching her before her loom—indoors in winter, out on the open porch in summertime—he would follow the tapestry of color and design rising from the bottom up, almost before his eyes. It was exciting to him to see the pattern unfold. She told him what her mother had told her, how it was important when you made a design to put in a tiny outlet to leave space so inspiration wouldn't be closed off for the next rug she designed.

Although many Navajo women worked from patterns set down for them by the traders, Alice Gorman, like other weavers who worked at home, used no drawings or patterns for her rugs. The mathematically precise designs were in her head, and she was guided by what she felt was inherently right. Soon her rugs began to achieve a reputation. The Babbitts' well-known trading post in Flagstaff, Arizona gave her a contract to supply as many as she could because the Babbitt brothers believed that her rugs would command a wide market. She proceeded to involve the women of Chinle. Some were expert weavers. Others had never woven before, but she taught them. They learned to shear their

Mary Peshlakai, Carl's aunt, ca. 1918.

own sheep, selecting the finest strands for their looms. They learned how to clean the wool, card it, spin it, and weave it. Alice helped them design the rugs, taught them how to shape them and keep them even. "It's important for you to be good," she told them. They were working in a commercial trade. They were selling a valuable commodity that people wanted, and this would help support their families, their children and grandchildren.

Other weavers with rugs to sell would come into Nelson Gorman's trading post with their husbands and children. The woman invariably carried the rug she had woven, for it was not only her work, it was her property. The sheep, the home, and all its utensils were her responsibility, hers to control according to Navajo tradition. As for the Navajo man, the cattle, the horses, and the paraphernalia of the ranch belonged to him. This was not entirely true of the Gormans, for Nelson was a businessman, an occupation out of the ordinary for most Navajos. His wife helped him in his trade and shared some of his responsibilities. There was no distinct division of property between Alice and Nelson. Carl never heard them quarrel over ownership of things; his parents felt that everything simply belonged to the family.

In the early 1900s, Navajo rugs were commonly sold by the pound, depending on the quality, as judged by the traders. But after a while traders stopped buying the rugs on that basis. Some Navajos were wetting the rugs, dampening them overnight, to make them heavier. Nelson Gorman set what he felt was the correct and proper price according to the quality, which he and Alice determined after examining the rugs carefully. Payment was primarily in merchandise, or the trader's "chip" money, small metal chips with the name of the trading post and the value stamped on them. There was very little haggling. Gorman's integrity was unquestioned.

The year 1916 was a turning point in the life of the Gorman family. Alice's sister, Bahajibah, died of tuberculosis. The disease was widespread on the Navajo reservation. She left five children. As the oldest girl, and the children's "shima yazzie" (little mother), Alice accepted her responsibility to take the children into her home. It was a household bulging at the walls. In addition to her sister's children and her own, Alice's younger brothers, Fred, Frank, and Paul Peshlakai, were living with them. They would all be there until the next year when a number, including Carl, would go off to boarding school. Fortunately, most of the children were out on the ranch all day, the older ones working on the farm, with the animals, or in the alfalfa fields.

That same year, Nelson Gorman decided to build "the big house." He had been thinking about it for a long time. Now, with the tumult of the many children about him, he knew there was no alternative. Several miles west of his trading post, members of the Táchii'nii clan, to which his wife belonged, held rights to a large parcel of land. It was given to Alice. Her father was Táchii'nii, and when she asked for the land it was given to her. Nelson Gorman found a beautiful clearing, brought in workmen, and began the construction of his new home. The large building with a high attic was made of blocks of rough-hewn stone. Inside were six rooms with oak floors and high ceilings, heated by two black, round wood stoves, one in the living room, and the other in the kitchen. There was no electricity in Chinle then or in fact, for many years to come. Rooms were lighted by kerosene lamps and in later years, lamps that burned gasoline. Nelson Gorman had planned a broad, wooden porch across the front, but during the First World War, with a shortage of supplies, he couldn't get lumber or nails, so the porch waited.

It was a huge establishment for Alice Gorman to take care of. Everyone pitched in. The children helped with the cooking, and they would all go out with her into the fields beyond the house to pick corn, melon, pumpkins. Members of the Peshlakai family came often. Her sister, Mary, born of one of Peshlakai's other wives, a lovely serious girl in her teens, would come on occasion to help her, especially when there was illness with the younger children. It was her way of showing her feelings of closeness, a feeling Navajos express not so much in words as in action. With Nelson Gorman's business affairs prospering, and a large household teeming with life, this was a good time.

THREE

Carl Gorman had a happy childhood on his father's ranch. He took special care of the abandoned lambs, and he had his own pet bull and his favorite horses. Living close to animals, loving them, he had no fear of any of them. When Carl was nine years old, his father was raising a stud, called Diamond, which was exceptionally mean. Carl was determined to prove his bravery to everyone. He persuaded his young brother, Wallace, to go with him. They found the horse lying down, jumped on it, and began to ride it around. A couple of the cowhands yelled for them to get off or they'd be killed! But they stayed on. It was a triumph for Carl, before the men. Even more important, he proved to his father he was as good at riding horses as he was at drawing them.

A strong relationship grew up between the young boy and his tall, lean, hard-working father. They rode together, driving cattle and making long treks from Chinle to the old saw mill on Ganado Ridge, or past Many Farms to Round Rock and back. Alice Gorman took care of the trading post while they were gone. They talked to each other in Navajo on these trips, although Carl's mother always insisted they speak English at home. For Carl, the growing identity with his father was a growing identity with the land, with the richness of the Navajo countryside, with a sense of the beauty that surrounded them. It would remain with Carl all his life.

These early years for Carl were a time of "walking in beauty," a free-and-easy time. He had found a love for art and for music, associated with his mother in her teachings. He was beginning to learn about his heritage and his Navajo culture as it came down to him through his father. The impressions would be lasting. They would be the foundation upon which his adult life and philosophy were based, through years of trial, hardship, even privation, through the ordeal of making his way in both the alien Anglo world and his own Navajo realm.

One memorable day, when Carl was still quite young, his father took him on an exploration of Canyon de Chelly. The time was late spring. They left on horseback in the early morning, their canteens filled with water, a lunch of dried peaches, cheese, nuts, and bread packed for them by Carl's mother. They soon left the familiar, dusty road that ran past the trading post, turning onto the packed dirt track that took them directly into the canyon. They moved along the riverbed that was to be their "highway" for a while. The base was firm, the sand tamped down by wagons and horses which had preceded them for days since the rains stopped. It was dangerous to come here alone, unless one knew his way. Quicksand, deep dry sand, and flash floods made the canyon hazardous.

Nelson Gorman waved his arm toward a narrow track of sand, at the edge of the riverbed. That was quicksand over there, he said. To the young boy it looked like any other area of sand. The two remained on the main track, a good fifty feet away. There were two things that everyone should know about quicksand, his father went on: first, where it was, and second that you always treated it with respect and stayed away.

"Do people get caught in the quicksand?" his son asked. Just the past year, the father said, he had seen a whole Navajo family standing away from the edge of the quicksand, just standing there and watching. The family wagon was sinking down into the sand; they unhitched the horse just in time. There was nothing more they could do. They stood there for a long time, he said, looking down. "They should have known where it was," he said. "They should have avoided it." He was bringing the point home firmly to his son.

The canyon began to narrow, the cliffs rising five to six hundred feet above them, their multicolored sandstone facades of red, orange, brown, laced downward from the top with long dark streaks, like ancient melted drippings frozen forever into place. From time to time, the two on horseback would leave the riverbed and make tracks through a bright green world of trees, plants, and flowers. Occasionally they saw a hogan nearby, a grazing horse, a flock of sheep. Against the sheltering base of a cliff, a Navajo was planting his corn in separate tilled mounds of earth. It was in the tradition of their ancestors, who had lived here for centuries, planting their corn, tending their sheep, living in close contact to the land they loved. In the winter, when the snows came, they would move to the winter hogan up on the mesa. Carl could hear the faint tinkling of bells. Sheep were grazing scattered high up the rocky path. His father liked to talk about the people who came before them. They moved with the seasons, he said, and took things as they came. They lived in harmony with nature, finding beauty in it, accepting. They made their lives adjust to all things, the good and the bad.

Carl learned about things of the past from his father. Nelson Gorman's own father, a medicine man in the Chinle region, had been respected and extremely learned. He would tell his son Nelson the old legends as he had heard them from his father. That was the way Navajo history had been "recorded." There was no written language, and hence no books to read it from. These historical stories were called legends because they were spoken, told by mouth, from generation to generation.

It was in these legends and old stories, Carl was reminded by his father, that he could learn the history of their past. In later years, Carl would find confirmation in the words and testimony of other Navajos whose knowledge he respected.

In this cherished land between their four sacred mountains, his father said to him, the ancestors of the Navajos worked their land, saw their families grow, took part in their ceremonies that had been brought to them by the Holy Ones. They had a religion that was a deep part of their daily lives.

But a profound change came over their lives during the sixteenth century when the Spaniards appeared in the Southwest. Navajos long recounted with bitterness how these white men appeared, mounted on horseback, wrapped in metal armor and bearing guns, in their relentless search for gold and silver. With them came their priests, determined to convert the native "heathen savages," and often more ruthless than the military itself.

Before the arrival of the white man, Athapascan-speaking clans, now referred to as Navajo, occupied territory adjacent to the village-dwelling Pueblo Indians. Navajo legends claim that their people occupied the area within the four sacred mountains for many centuries before the coming of the Spaniards. When the Spanish attacks took place against the Pueblo villages, many Navajos joined in the fight against the white invaders.

The harsh, disrupting influence of the Spanish soldiers and their militant priests served to keep the peoples of the region in a state of fear and turmoil. For many years to come, the Navajos felt that their land, their animals, their very lives were at stake. Besides the Spanish, the Navajos had other enemies to contend with. The Utes were engaged in slave trade for the Spanish, who were masters of the policy of divide and conquer, pitting tribe against tribe, and at the same time getting slaves for their mines in Mexico as well as for their homes.

The Navajo retaliated by fighting not only the Spanish but those tribes who were slaving and those Pueblos who submitted to Spanish rule. Many Pueblo people, some from Jemez and elsewhere, fled to the Navajos for refuge from Spanish domination. The Navajos began to take possession of the sheep, cattle, and horses that were left behind by the Spaniards or captured in raids, regarding these animals as gifts from the Holy People, gifts that could provide them with precious food and clothing. Most important, with the horses they captured, the Navajos had a new mobility and strength in mounting their raids. They felt justified in these raids when they saw their lands invaded, their homes and families attacked by the Spaniards and other Indian tribes, their children stolen from them and taken away into slavery. The Navajo raids and counterattacks continued intermittently through the eighteenth and nineteenth centuries.

A story that Carl learned from his father was one his people told about the courage of their ancestors in the face of cruel death. At a junction of towering cliffs in Canyon de Chelly, the main canyon turns off to the right, and the narrower bed of Canyon del Muerto, "the Canyon of Death," winds out of sight to the left. It got its name from a grisly incident. A troop of vengeful Spanish soldiers came up this canyon in the winter of 1804–5, with their horses and guns, bound on destroying all the Navajo people they could find there. They murdered twenty-five women and children who took refuge on a rock ledge, the place now known as Massacre Cave. The tale was of the brave young Navajo girl who was on this ledge high on the cliff. One of the Spanish soldiers had climbed up to the place where they were all hiding. The young girl came forward bravely and pushed him, and they both fell together to their death in the canyon below.

By the middle of the nineteenth century, as the Navajos told it, a new enemy appeared on the scene. In 1846, the United States government declared war on Mexico and acquired the lands which were to become territories of Arizona and New Mexico. American settlers came to stake out their own ranches and homesteads. Once again, the Navajos felt that the land between their four sacred mountains was in danger of being taken away from them. They saw the settlers plowing the very grasslands on which the Navajo herds had grazed for centuries. Despite their protests, an army fort was built in the middle of the Navajo land to protect the settlers. There was continual raiding and bloodshed. The histories of the Pueblo people and of the Americans relate in detail the hostilities of the Navajo raiders. But the Navajo people themselves felt that the actions of their warriors were justified. For generations they had been attacked by Mexicans, by the Utes who had been urged on by the Spanish, and now by the Americans, who had invaded their lands. They retaliated in mounting anger.

The year 1864 was crucial. Far to the east, the white man's armies of the North and South were engaged in the Civil War. Still, the military decision was made that soldiers should be sent to Navajo country to crush and capture the people living there. It was winter when a troop of soldiers appeared in Canyon de Chelly under the command of Colonel "Kit" Carson. His orders were to round up all the Navajos. They were to be taken from their land, from their homes, and from the protection of the Sacred Mountains. They were to be marched to Fort Defiance, and from there 300 miles away to Fort Sumner. Thousands of Navajo men, women, and children had been rounded up. Many tried to escape, and some did, searching for refuge in distant caves and remote canyons. Kit Carson and his soldiers began to round up the last ones who had fled to the remote recesses of the canyons. En route they killed the livestock, destroyed the hogans, poisoned the food and water, and burned the beautiful peach orchards to the ground. Anyone who resisted was killed.

There is a massive fortress-like cliff at the junction of Canyon del Muerto and a smaller canyon. The canyon walls are high, dark, sheer, oppressive. It is called Fortress Rock, "Tselaa," by the Navajos. The old Navajos tell how several hundred of the people, fleeing for their lives from the soldiers, found refuge on the broad top of the cliff. The winter had become bitter cold. The people pulled up their ladders and poles behind them so the enemy could not follow. The Navajo soldiers had brought up their wounded, carrying them up the long, narrow trails, 900 feet to the top. As weeks of suffering passed, there was no more food left, no more water. The Navajos went to work making a long rope of yucca plants and old Mexican ropes. They fastened jugs to the end of the long rope. Then they climbed down the cliff with it, and they hoisted water up from a pool at the bottom, so close to the feet of the sleeping white soldiers that they could almost touch them. Their bravery gained a few days. The tragic end came when they had to surrender, because their women and children were starving. Along with many others, this story seeped into the history and consciousness of the Navajo people. It told of their ordeal and of their struggles to survive against injustice and force, against prejudice and greed. Those who escaped could continue to tell it.

Nearly 7,000 Navajos were eventually rounded up on Navajo land. But there were many, 2,000 or more, who escaped. A number found a sanctuary in Grand Canyon and in Bear's Ear Mountain, "Shashjaa'," in Utah. Carl's own grandfather, Peshlakai, had the opportunity to escape, but he chose to stay with his family. He had seen his father and mother taken in fear, along with his brothers and sisters. He went with them. He was young and strong, and he would take care of them, he said.

The terror known as the Long Walk began. The Navajos were herded like animals and taken down to Fort Defiance. Those who came back from the ordeal were to tell and retell of the shame, the fear, the horror of being harshly uprooted and expelled from their sacred homeland. With alien soldiers guarding them at gunpoint, prodding them cruelly, they were forced to march for hundreds of miles in the hot sun, tramping in the dust, blistered by the wind. Several hundred died on the way. If a Navajo fell and was still alive, the people tried to carry him. If he held up the march too long, or if he was too ill, the soldiers pushed him to one side leaving him to die in the ditch. After walking some three hundred miles, the people finally arrived at the barren, windswept reservation on the banks of the Pecos River in eastern New Mexico.

The place was called Bosque Redondo by the Mexicans. Nearby was the recently established Fort Sumner, where the American soldiers, who were to guard the Navajos, were quartered. In the four years the Navajos were in this place of hardship and suffering, of inadequate food and shelter and lack of clothing, more than 2,000 of their people died of dysentery, pneumonia, and malnutrition.

The first Indians at the Bosque Redondo camp were a group of over four hundred Mescalero Apaches from southeastern New Mexico. The Navajos were put to work with them, constructing adobe buildings for the army. It was a military blunder. Conflict sprang up between the two tribes.

In the harsh environment, the people struggled to survive. They planted crops each year, but the soil was too dry for farming. Irrigation canals from the Pecos River were constructed, but the corn, wheat, and melon crops never matured; the precious young corn was devoured by cutworms. The people lived through fierce heat and drought in the summer. The winters were bitter beyond endurance for many. The people lived in holes in the ground. They would dig as deep as they could without the walls of earth caving in, and then they made a covering of brush, scraps of canvas, sometimes animal hides. The weak could not survive the damp, ill-heated holes for four severe winters.

But the ill and half-starved people did not give up hope of returning to their Dine' bikéyeh, their Navajo land. Reports of their plight, and of their determination, went back to Washington. A Peace Commission came to the Bosque Redondo in May of 1868 to confer with the Navajo leaders. Soon afterwards, General William T. Sherman met in council with the Navajos. Their chief spokesman was Barboncito. He spoke eloquently of the tragedies that had afflicted his people, of how many had died, and of their animals, too. He saw no purpose in so much death. The only wish of his people was to return to their country. He succeeded in convincing the general and the Peace Commission that the Navajos should return to the lands that had formerly belonged to them.

An agreement was reached between the peace commissioners and the Navajo leaders. The people could go back to their land. A federal agency would be set up at Fort Defiance; the livestock would be replenished; and schools were to be set up for all children between the ages of six and sixteen, with a house and a teacher for every thirty

Carl and his father in alfalfa field, Chinle farm, 1915.

children. The treaty was signed on June 1, 1868 by ten representatives
of the U.S. government and twenty-nine Navajo leaders.

Within two weeks, the exodus from the Bosque Redondo began. The
people headed back to their country between the Four Sacred Mountains,
to the open plateau lands, to the mesas, to the pines of Chuska Forest
and the cherished Canyon de Chelly. Most went back to their own
homesteads. They brought with them their meager resources of horses
and mules, sheep and goats. Within the next few years the government
kept its promise to issue some 15,000 sheep and goats. The Navajos
began to rebuild their herds, cultivate their fields, build new homes and
corrals, clean their springs, the precious waterholes, and perform their
ceremonies once more.

Many more details of this history would be known to Carl in later
years. But already, through his father, he was learning of his people,
beginning to understand their love of the land, something of their suffering, their hardships, and their ability to endure.

Now the land was at peace. Carl felt it as he and his father moved
up the narrow Canyon del Muerto on horseback past the mounds of
growing corn, past the peach orchards in a birth of first flowering. The
soft, unexpected humming of bees surrounded them. There was a peace
here beyond compare, and the young boy responded to it. He felt a part

of this land, of the people who were living here, of all the people who had ever lived here.

At a quick turn in the canyon trackway, the wonder of Antelope Ruins was before him. People had lived here eight or nine hundred years before. The sandstone remnants of the small rectangular homes they had built nestled for protection beneath a sheer and overwhelming cliff. The broken circular wall of an ancient ceremonial kiva stood out in the foreground, as if to tell one to pay attention, that here people of a village far distant in time lived and prayed and held festive rites long before any white man came to any part of this land. The people were gone, but Carl, in the warmth of the sunlit walls that morning, could still imagine them, still hear the sounds of their voices and laughter echoing in and out of those time-worn walls.

Carl turned to gaze toward the great cliff wall to the left of the ruins. There, in clear definition, was a series of splendid antelopes, colorfully painted in deep shades of brown pigment. Full of eternal life, never slowing, as they leaped along the face of the wall. Carl gasped at the sight. The antelopes stirred his imagination as nothing had ever done before. He continued to stare upward with fascination. The paintings may have been made in the early nineteenth century by Navajos who knew the importance of the antelopes to the Anasazi, who killed them for food and for the skins which would keep them warm in the winter.

In the years that followed, this magic area was Carl's playground. He returned to Canyon de Chelly many times, alone on horseback, searching for new ruins, looking for the pictographs that might be found hidden away on the high, secluded walls of the canyon. He discovered hundreds of them, never tiring of the search. But he always would come back to these antelopes. Then he would go home and draw them.

FOUR

Carl's golden childhood ended abruptly when he was ten years old. His parents felt it was time for him to attend a school away from home. His mother objected to sending him to a government school. She had heard too many reports of the harsh conditions, the iron-handed regime, the poor food, the punishment that went with the teaching. She chose to send him to a new Protestant school that had been set up by the Christian Dutch Reform movement at Rehoboth Mission, some dozen miles east of Gallup, New Mexico. It was over a hundred miles from their home in Chinle. No resistance on Carl's part could do any good. Both his parents said he had to go. Other children were going too, including his sister Mary, and Frank Peshlakai, his uncle, who was of the same age.

Nelson Gorman decided to risk taking them all to school in his Model T Ford. In this not-quite-dependable vehicle, they managed to travel the long, dusty, winding dirt road to Gallup, and then along the main road to the mission. Nelson Gorman wished Carl and the other children well, and he left for home.

The time at the mission school was a difficult one for Carl. He was a tall, gangly youth, approaching adolescence, with a natural spirit and an air of rebellion about him from the beginning. Very different from the other three children, he found it exceptionally hard settling down to a regimen that was so alien to him. The grim living conditions, the sparse meals, and the punishments were hardly different from those to be found in most government schools.

The students slept in a dormitory—a huge, long room with high ceilings and bare wooden floors. Each had his own small cot, with an army blanket to keep him warm. The winters were bitterly cold. Carl's cot was close to one steam radiator. Each night he would release the safety valve to make the room warmer. The principal, making his rounds, found the valve missing one night. He searched the dormitory until he found it in Carl's bed; first he slapped the boy hard and then asked him to explain what the valve was doing there. In Navajo fashion, Carl said nothing.

The principal, Mr. Bosscher, was tall and heavy-set and wore dark, loose-fitting civilian clothes. In describing him in a letter home, Carl wrote that "he looked horrible." At Rehoboth there were usually six or seven teachers, mostly women. They wore dresses down to their ankles. Carl's description of them was terse: "They were mean as scorpions."

The students ate in a large, cold dining hall at long tables. Their diet was bread and oatmeal for breakfast; bread, water, and a very occasional egg for lunch; beans, beef, or pork for dinner.

During the week, the boys wore jeans, shirts, and boots. But on Sunday, they always had to wear a gray wool uniform, with the tunic tightly buttoned to the neck, and a short visor cap. The jacket had to remain buttoned as they sat upright in church, on hard seats, for several hours. If they fell asleep, or if they so much as nodded, a matron poked them briskly in the back with a long stick.

According to schedule, the students got up every morning at 6:00 A.M. After cleaning up, they sat at attention while the matron read from the Bible and prayed. At breakfast, they prayed before they ate, then someone read from the Bible, and they prayed again. In every class, the teacher prayed first before they began their studies in grammar, figures, inspirational readings. At the end of each class the teacher read the Bible and prayed again. It was stifling and overwhelming. The only protection against this religious bombardment was for Carl and the other Navajo children to turn it off and ignore it as much as possible.

Sunday was the worst day. They marched to church in their tight uniforms. They were forced to sit out the long hours while the preacher, high on the platform above them, ranted interminably. The sermon was consistently a harsh tirade against all sinful actions. The students felt only the hardness of the preacher's tone; they never understood the words he actually spoke.

Of all the days in the week, only Saturday was left for the children. It was a free day. They could go out into the open fields and play baseball, or go deep into the woods and pick piñon nuts in season. Carl found time to draw. He would carry pencil and paper with him, and put down images that stimulated his imagination. He drew a picture of Church Rock, the splendid sandstone formation that loomed against the sky, cathedral-like, some miles to the north. He showed it proudly to a teacher; she admired it and bought the drawing from him for fifteen cents.

School lasted nine months of the year. Nelson Gorman would pick up the children in Gallup and take them home in the family wagon. There was Carl, his uncle Frank, his sister Mary, along with his younger brother Wallace and his cousins Martha and Luke, who came to Rehoboth in the second year. They looked forward to returning to the big house. Carl worked all summer on the ranch and in the alfalfa fields.

Carl Gorman was at Rehoboth during World War I. The students were aware of its existence because they were on very meager food rations. Because of the war, government schools were rationed for food. The Christian missionary schools observed the same policy. Carl and a boy named Franklin worked in the kitchen. They looked forward to emptying the slop can at the pig sty. They were so starved they went through it for anything edible—a piece of bread, apple peels, a scrap of meat. In the aftermath of the war, through the winter of 1918–19, the flu epidemic cut its devastating swath across America and most of the Western world. It reached the remote mission school at Rehoboth. Of the hundred or more children, only six were not stricken and several died. Carl was one of the few who remained well. He spent his time helping the nurses take care of those who were sick.

The flu epidemic reached the small Navajo community of Chinle and Nelson Gorman's trading post. He and his wife Alice became ill. Nelson Gorman lost two of his sisters.

It was a time of bitter blows. The epidemic struck hard, not only at the health of the people but at all business activity. The revenues at the trading post went down sharply. Worst of all, the McKinley First State Bank in Gallup, in which Nelson Gorman kept his funds, closed its doors. He lost $20,000, all his savings. In addition, he lost his life insurance. His health still impaired, he decided to close the trading post. Alice was grateful that their lives had been spared. With Nelson's agreement, she gave the post and the home attached to the Presbyterian church, their first permanent building and meeting place.

The flu epidemic had come swiftly upon the reservation. The Navajos had their own explanation of its origin. Just before the epidemic, at Antelope Spring near Jeddito, the Navajos were holding a large Yei-bi-chei ceremony. A group of Hopi Indians came by and wanted to join in the dance. The Navajos let them. They sang and danced, and shortly after, the flu swept through the Navajo country. The people blamed the Hopis for it, convinced that it was their dancing at the ceremony that had caused the terrible disease.

Of all the conditions at the Rehoboth Mission school, the worst was the staff's determination, typical of Indian education at that time, to force the Navajo children to become completely anglicized, to dress like Americans, to think like Americans, and to speak English only. Virtually all the children had come from traditional Navajo homes. They were comfortable speaking Navajo, and they did so whenever they could. But when they were caught at it, they were punished, sometimes harshly.

Speaking English was no effort for Carl, for he had always heard it at home. But he wanted to learn more Navajo and speak it with his friends at school, and he fiercely resented being forbidden to do so at Rehoboth. The more he was caught and punished, the more he reacted. He made it a principle of rebellion that he would speak Navajo every moment he could. Carl had known discipline in his home, but with compassion and understanding. He flared at the cold, unbending discipline of these "outsiders" who thundered at him with their authority, and whom he could never respect.

Carl's rebellion reached the point where he openly defied a teacher in class. Refusing to answer in English, he roared back at him insultingly in Navajo.

The principal resolved that this time a severe beating would not be enough to teach Carl Gorman a lesson. He had the boy locked into a basement room. The building was all stone. It was the middle of winter and the walls were cold and clammy. Mr. Bosscher had Carl chained in a corner against the wall. For a week he was kept there in chains with nothing but chunks of bread and a bowl of water for nourishment. When they finally released him, it was with a grim admonishment: "Now perhaps you'll be obedient."

From that moment on, Carl was determined to run away, waiting only for the right time. He intended to slip out alone. Frank, his young uncle, found out and insisted on coming with him. It was the cold month of February 1920. Late one afternoon, they left Rehoboth in a hurry with no food. They had not gone far when Carl's younger brother Wallace came running after them. They tried to send him back, but he insisted on coming too. The three headed northward over the mountain for fifteen or more miles until they reached a small place called Gibson, the site of a big coal mine and a railroad siding. A heavy, cold rain was falling. The boys crawled into a boxcar, slept a few hours, then started out again before dawn. Early in the morning, they crossed the Rio Puerco, and Frank fell into a deep place getting thoroughly soaked. Carl worried about him the entire day as they made their way over rough terrain. Finally they reached Fort Defiance, and Carl remembered a missionary there named Clark whom his mother had known. The three were famished; Carl hoped that the missionary would feed them. He wasn't at home, but his Navajo interpreter took them in. His wife fed them and gave them a place to sleep.

The missionary returned late and found out about the boys. Carl

Frank Peshlakai, Carl, his brother Wallace, Rehoboth School, New Mexico, 1917.

overheard him saying that he'd let them stay for the night, but he was going to take them back to Rehoboth in the morning.

It was three o'clock when Carl and the others slipped out of the house as fast as they could and headed for Chinle. The sun came up when they were on their way to Sawmill. A white man driving a team of horses came along. He picked them up and took them that far. Then they continued across country. They had to traverse two mountains. The second was packed solidly with snow. It was dark by the time they reached it. They built a big fire and managed to keep warm during the night, but they had no food. In the morning, Carl suggested they make a detour in order to reach his paternal grandmother's home. He thought that they would stay there for a while, but she was gone. She had already moved, with her sheep, to her winter camp some distance away.

The boys had no alternative now but to go on to Chinle. They arrived there on the third evening of their escape. They reached the Chinle wash below the trading post. Carl saw his younger brother Steve out there, chasing the family goats, rounding them up for the night. The three boys were desperately hungry, but they were afraid to go to the big house. Carl's brother Wallace took the initiative. He said he was so hungry he didn't care what would happen and he couldn't wait. He led the way up the porch, and they all went inside.

Carl's father and mother were both there, sitting at the large oak dining table near the warm stove. They were surprised at the sight of the three ragged, hungry boys standing sheepishly before them. The first questions were what had happened, what were the children doing there.

Now Carl poured out his story, how he'd been mistreated for speaking Navajo, then severely punished, and finally confined in a cold stone room for a week with both legs chained. Alice listened to her son's tale in disbelief. It was inconceivable to her that the mission people—good Christian people—would have abused him so. Carl's father listened in silence.

The next day Carl repeated his story to his father, in exactly the same detail. Nelson Gorman believed his son. He wrote a letter to Principal Bosscher at Rehoboth. The principal wrote back at once, putting all the blame on Carl, as always. He called him the worst, the most rebellious student he had ever known. Nelson Gorman decided he would not send his son back. The other two boys, however, had not been involved in disciplinary problems, though they had chosen to leave with Carl, and Nelson Gorman insisted they return to school. He took them by wagon to Gallup. There he met with Bosscher, who had come to pick up the children. Bosscher became extremely vocal in blaming Carl for everything that had happened. Nelson Gorman reacted angrily. He came to his son's defense, and he warned the principal that he'd better treat the other children with care, or he would be held personally accountable.

All his life, Carl would be grateful for his father's belief in him. Three decades after the incident, when he painted a portrait of his father in oils, he still spoke of his gratitude.

At about the same time, in the 1950s, when he was in Gallup, Carl came across a doctor who was still working at Rehoboth. For a brief moment they talked about the mission school. Then the doctor said to Carl sanctimoniously, "It made a man out of you." Carl shook his head, "No, it didn't," he said. "The Marines made a man out of me."

FIVE

The problem of future schooling for Carl was a serious one. He was full of hatred for the treatment he had received at the religious institution. The only alternative left now was a government school. But where? Education, on or off the Navajo reservation, was not succeeding for the majority of Indian students.

When the Navajos returned to their homeland after the Long Walk and the bitter four-year confinement at Fort Sumner, one of the major stipulations of the Treaty of 1868 was that the Navajos were to compel all their children between the ages of six and sixteen to attend school; the government would provide a classroom and a competent teacher for every thirty students.

The program was a dismal failure. It was late in starting, and the policy of enforcement did not work. A small day school was opened at Fort Defiance in 1870. A handful of students came. They were handed out uniforms, and then they left, never to come back. Nothing else was done by the Indian Service until 1883 when the first boarding school was set up in Fort Defiance. That, too, closed its doors in a short time when students failed to come.

By now, the missionaries of various denominations were coming onto the reservation, determined to convert the "heathen" to a Christian way of life. Given government contracts to do so, they began to set up schools alongside the new missions, all in widely separated sections of the reservation. There was a Methodist school near Farmington, a Franciscan school at St. Michael's opened in 1898, a Presbyterian school at Ganado in 1902, and a few years later, the Christian Dutch Reform Church school at Rehoboth, to which Carl had been sent. A limited number of students came, out of the thousands who needed schooling. Unlike Carl's grandfather, Peshlakai, most Navajo parents were reluctant to send their children away from home, away from their family life, the warmth and closeness of it, the culture in which they had been nurtured. Also, they were needed to tend the sheep.

The roads were bad, the winters severe, and the children remained at the boarding schools for months at a time, usually the entire school year. In addition, the policy in the federal schools on the reservation was to expedite "acculturation" as speedily as possible. The children were forbidden to speak Navajo. At Ganado, where Carl's youngest brother, Steve, had gone, boys were punished if they spoke in their native language, by being dressed up in girl's clothes. The children were reminded interminably that they must learn to dress, to speak, to think like white people. They were to forget their Navajo upbringing, their Navajo way of life, which they had been taught was beautiful and good and given to them by their own Holy People. All this was in order to be like the white man and pray to the white man's god. But many of the children, coming from traditional homes, had been taught by their parents and grandparents to remember that the white man had been their enemy, that he had subjected them to life on a reservation, that he had been responsible for the terrors of the Long Walk, that he had brought cruelty and injustice into their lives, that he had deprived them of their land, of their freedom, of the right to many of their ancient ceremonies and religious rites, and that he still considered them "savages and heathens."

Off the reservation, there were a number of government schools. Most were far away: the Sherman Institute in Riverside, California; Grand Junction and Fort Lewis in Colorado; Haskell Institute in Kansas; Santa Fe Indian School in New Mexico; and one in Albuquerque. Of all these, Carl's father decided that the best place for him to go, as well as the closest, would be the Indian School in Albuquerque. It had a good reputation, an all-around curriculum, and a reputation for being fair to the students. Also, Carl's father knew Mr. Perry, the new superintendent, who had worked among the Navajos before he was transferred to the Albuquerque Indian School.

In the fall of 1921, Carl Gorman, aged fourteen, said goodbye to his parents. An official from the B.I.A. came from the Chinle government office to pick up Carl and take him to Fort Defiance. A group of Navajo boys and girls were there, brought in from different parts of the reservation. They went by truck to Gallup and were let off at the railroad station. The Navajo students all crowded together in the back coach of the train. But they were moved out by the porter who insisted it was not for "them." As the train stopped at Laguna on its way to Albuquerque, another train smashed into it. The rear coach, made of wood, was completely demolished. Had they remained there, all of the students would have been killed or injured. After remaining at Laguna all night until the track was cleared, they arrived safely in Albuquerque the next day.

The Indian School was on the western outskirts of town, surrounded by farms, where many of the students were to work. Several of the buildings were of red brick. The dormitories were two-story wooden army barracks. Carl was relieved to find the living conditions far better than at Rehoboth. The personnel in charge were military oriented and the school was run on military lines—firm, often strict, but eminently fair. The boys dressed in uniforms only on Sunday. The rest of the week they wore casual clothes. They slept on metal-framed army cots. Mr. Perry, the head of the school, held inspections every Sunday. Dormitories had to be in perfect shape. On the drill field, the boys would line up in military order for inspection, saluting the flag while the school band played "The Star-Spangled Banner."

All classes were taught in English. There were more than a thousand students here, many from different Southwest Indian tribes: Navajo, Apache, Hopi, and the other Pueblos. They were allowed to speak their own languages when they chose. It was a new milieu for Carl, with a sense of freedom he had never known at Rehoboth. Nor could he complain about the food, a plentiful army diet, supervised by a dietician.

Even with the advantages of the new school, Carl was still a youngster who had trouble settling down. He liked to play the role of rebel, trying to impress his comrades with his spirit of independence. But a fortunate thing happened. A Navajo upperclassman, Justin Shirley, came to him. He was a slim, serious student of eighteen, secure, sure of himself. He literally took Carl under his direction, telling him to settle down, cut out the rough talk. That wasn't the Navajo way, he pointed out. Carl began to look up to Justin and accept his advice. He had found an authority figure he could respect. In true Navajo fashion, Justin became the "older brother" Carl Gorman needed badly.

Carl was never a serious student, the academic subjects holding no attraction for him, but he managed to do enough studying to pass all his courses. His great interest was athletics. He excelled in track, baseball, boxing, and especially football. When an injury sidelined him for a while, he concentrated on boxing. Determined to build himself up, he saw an advertisement for the "Earl E. Liederman Physical Culture" correspondence course and sent for it. Along with the course, he received an exercise cable. He worked with it continually, developing the strong chest and shoulder muscles that not only helped his boxing but later served him in good stead when he became a Marine in World War II. Carl was a natural boxer, strong, springy. He was scheduled to meet the best fighter in the school, a senior with a reputation for toughness. Carl came to Justin Shirley for advice. He was in trouble, he said to his mentor, afraid he was going to get licked. There was nothing to be afraid about, Justin Shirley said. "He's only got two hands like you," and he added laughing, "Just be faster."

When the fight took place, Justin Shirley had a work assignment at school and couldn't be present. Carl came to him that night exultant because he had won. "I didn't forget a word you said! I licked him cold!" he yelled, grabbing his friend in a bear hug. "You should have seen the look when I beat him to the punch—every time!"

There was very little money for Carl as a student. His father sent him some from time to time, but it was never much; he was still recovering from the loss of his trading post and his savings. The B.I.A. gave the students a chance to work on the farms during school time, for which they earned a modest sum. The school authorities held their earnings, then doled them out to the students on request. Besides working on the farm, Carl went into town on Saturdays and worked as a handyman.

Carl began to mature in the environment of the Albuquerque School. Boys of the other tribes, as well as Navajos, liked him. He had charm and an easy manner, and they looked up to him. There were class parties with dancing and music once a month, with girls who lived in the dorms on the other side of the campus. These were the early years of Prohibition, and the school discipline was strict. The authorities cracked down on the least drinking.

Of all the people Carl came to know in Albuquerque, his favorite was the "Chili Lady," a kind Mexican woman who had a chili stand just outside the school. She sold soda pop, candy, and pie as well as chili to the students. She enjoyed them; they adored her. Her stand became a congregating place for them after school, especially in the evenings.

Mrs. Campa was captivated by Carl. She brought him home to her family, to meet her two sons and a daughter. She told him the story of how she had left Mexico. Her husband, a government officer at the time of Pancho Villa, had been killed, and she fled for her life with the children. In Albuquerque she set up this little business to support them and put them through school. They all went to the University of New Mexico. One of the brothers, Arthur Campa, became a professor of Spanish at the University of Colorado; his brother, David, went on to study law and eventually went to Washington, working for the Mexican government in the field of international law. Carl Gorman continued to be friends with the family for many years. He corresponded with the two brothers. Decades later, when Carl's son R. C. decided he wanted to go to Mexico and study art, he had difficulties getting into a school. It was David Campa who directly intervened and helped him be accepted by Mexico City College to study there, the first Navajo to do so.

In 1924 Carl's mother became very ill. The news that she had died came in a long letter from his younger brother Wallace. He wrote of how their mother had returned to the home where she had been born, surrounded by the green fields and the trees she loved. Wallace was with her one afternoon when it appeared to him that she was dying. He ran from the house to get help. Then he saw a coyote coming across his path. Here was the symbol of death, coming to someone in the family. Wallace ran back into the house, grabbed a rifle, rushed out to fire it over the head of the coyote, not to kill him but to frighten him away. Then he raced to get help. But when they got back, his mother was dead. She was not yet forty years old.

Carl could not go home for the funeral; the distance was too great. The school authorities suggested it might be wiser for him to remain, in view of the transportation problems. Carl had been physically apart from his mother for so many years, so involved in his adolescent activities, that the reports of her illness had not affected him deeply. He had always seen her in his mind as someone strong and positive in her thinking, in her religious faith. He felt sure she would get well. Now, in the certainty of her death, the separation between the two was complete. Carl was torn by the knowledge that he would never see her again. A solid influence was gone from his life. His mother had been a spiritual rudder to his course. With her gone, he felt isolated, adrift.

The one anchor for his emotions was in athletics, and in the next years at school, Carl put all his energies into them. He played on the Albuquerque Indian School football team that won the state championship two years in succession under Coach Jones, the formidable Okla-

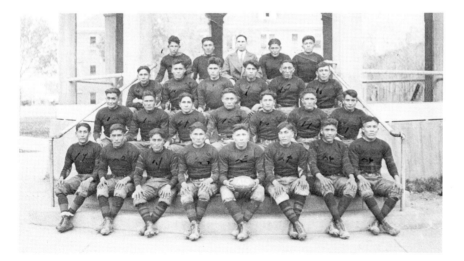

Albuquerque Indian School Football Squad; Carl in back row, second from right, 1927.

homa Indian, who was a man the boys never forgot. He was tough and fair. He drilled them with terse instructions on a blackboard, and he cared so much about his boys that in a game with Farmington, when rowdy spectators started throwing rocks at his Albuquerque team and one player got hit, Coach Jones pulled the team off the field and forfeited the game. For two years Carl was an all-state guard, selected twice as best player on the team. He also played baseball and basketball, boxed, wrestled, and ran the 220 and the 440.

At graduation time, Carl received a certificate. It was not truly a diploma; it did not say he had finished the twelfth grade or had graduated from high school. Instead, it stated that he had completed his course in farming, and that his schoolwork was satisfactory. Carl looked at the piece of paper in his hand. He reread the citation, "Satisfactory in Farming." He tore it up and threw the shreds of paper onto the school ground. He resented what he felt was a snub to him, to all the Indian students, that they were being put down because they were Indian, that the authorities didn't want to say, "Here is an educated Indian." All the boys at the school had learned a trade. They took part in athletics. They completed their academic courses. But they received no credit for these, no recognition. They were merely given certificates for the trades they had completed: "Satisfactory in Farming." It meant to Carl that they were being told they were really not educated. They had simply finished courses in a trade school.

Carl lost all interest in further education. The football team on which he excelled had played scrimmage games with the University of New Mexico and with Texas Christian University. Both universities offered Carl football scholarships, but he turned them down. At the age of twenty, when he might have felt a strong urge to strike out on his own, to see what the outside world was like, Carl chose to return to Chinle and to his father's ranch.

SIX

The 1920s were restless years for Carl Gorman. The ranch was no longer the source of joy he had known as a child, when he cared for the animals and roamed at will. Now it was a place where hard work was demanded in the heat of the day or under a whipping wind or in searing cold. But Carl had no desire to leave, no urge to look anywhere else for opportunity. He liked the companionship of the older cowhands, and he spent long hours after work gambling with them.

By the age of twenty-one, Carl Gorman was tall, rangy, inordinately handsome. The Navajo girls found him magnetic. He was a favorite at Squaw Dance ceremonials where the women would choose their partners, compelling them, according to the old ritual, to pay for the privilege of dancing with them. He appeared to have no favorites himself, preferring to say that he liked them all.

That phase came to a close when, at the age of twenty-two, Carl fell wildly in love with Adelle Katherine Brown, who was young, spirited, and pretty. She had just returned from the Indian School at Riverside, California with a certificate in home economics and was working for the Bureau of Indian Affairs at Chinle in a dull job as a cook. When Carl impetuously decided they ought to get married, she immediately accepted. It was 1930 and the depression had hit the Navajo reservation. The young couple went to live in a tiny frame house, close to the hogan compound that belonged to Adelle's family. In July 1931, their first son was born, Rudolph Carl Gorman. The depression deepened all over the country, but nowhere was it more seriously felt than among the Navajos. Unemployment was high, even for the able-bodied. The value of sheep, mainstay of the tribal economy, fell drastically; the demand for wool was nonexistent. Carl's father held onto his ranch, keeping as many of his herds as possible. But there was no money coming in, and he pared his working force to the bone.

Carl had a family to support. He borrowed an old truck from his father, and he went into business in partnership with his brother Wallace, hauling coal on contract for the government schools. Within the next two years, Carl's wife bore him two more children, Donna and Donald. The burdens and pressure of family life quickly took their toll on the youthful marriage. The disagreements between Carl and his wife became frequent, intense, disturbing.

There was an ever-growing need for money, with the larger family and the income from the trucking business diminishing. Carl found that a ready source of revenue existed for a man who had a truck at his disposal. The resistance to Prohibition was as strong among the Navajos on the reservation as it was among the populace throughout the rest of the United States. Their craving for alcohol was just as great, and the fact that its consumption was illicit, prohibited by the white man's law, made it all the more desirable. Carl was in Gallup with his truck, when a relative introduced him to "the trade." He was to deal with a Mexican-American coal miner who made a powerful brand of corn whiskey that everyone called White Mule. Carl bought it by the gallon, and then he proceeded to pour it into Coca-Cola bottles for distribution on the reservation. The demand always exceeded his supply, especially since he catered to the throngs of Navajos who gathered to participate in Squaw Dances and various ceremonials.

The business was lucrative for a time. It was against the law, Carl admitted, but a law that everyone flouted; he at least was bringing the money home for his family. The repeal of Prohibition in 1933 ended his illegal career. There were Navajos who continued their bootlegging business with steady customers on the reservation, for alcohol continued to be prohibited there, and the serving of liquor in the bordering towns was still forbidden to Indians.

Desperate for work, Carl finally succeeded in getting a job in the Soil Conservation Corps, under the Bureau of Land Management for the U.S. government. He was one of a hundred applying. The key to his employment was the fact that he spoke English better than the rest, and he was immediately assigned to work as an interpreter. His new job took him away from home a great deal, as he moved about the reservation on government assignments.

Carl enjoyed the newfound sense of freedom, of escape from the confines of a trying marital relationship. He had no regrets about being apart from Adelle. But he missed his companionship with little Rudy, his first-born son. The child looked up to his father with admiration.

Carl before his first marriage, Gallup, 1929.

Little Rudy Gorman, Chinle, 1932.

By the time he was four, he delighted Carl by beginning to draw with unusual skill.

On many occasions Rudy had watched his father sit down and draw for the pure enjoyment of it. Carl Gorman would have been the last person to say later he inspired or taught the boy how to be an artist. But Rudy began to imitate him. He would draw on every occasion he could. He would go out onto the dry riverbed of nearby Canyon de Chelly with a pointed stick in his hand and make pictures in the sand and mud. His great love was for autos and trucks of all sizes and variations. Perhaps it had something to do with the fact that his father was a driver of trucks, that he was such a welcome sight when he came rattling into the compound in his old truck after a long trip away.

When Rudy was seven or eight, he began to spend his summers with his father. For the boy, like Carl with his own father, the time spent was memorable. They were away from home together, up near Navajo Mountain in northern Arizona close to the Utah border. It was an exciting man's world for Rudy. His father let him hold the hot iron for branding cows. Rudy dipped sheep with his father. He watched his father gamble, thrilling to the shouts, the laughter, and his father's winning.

"I loved being out in the field with him, out in the open," he recalled later. "I grew up that way, and I've never lost it, a feeling for the land and the people. Wherever I go now, wherever I work—it can be thousands of miles away from the Reservation—I carry it with me. For the Navajo

48

culture, my feeling remains deep. A rich awareness and a belief in the Navajo way. I got a lot of that from my father."

Though Carl Gorman had been brought up by his mother in both Catholic and Episcopal religions, he was to renounce both. The harsh treatment he had received at the Rehoboth Mission School as a child turned him against Christianity, and he never practiced it. The influence of his father and the ceremonies he would often attend with his friends and their families brought to him in his youth an appreciation of his Navajo culture. While working in the stock reduction program, one of his Navajo co-workers was a medicine man at Kaibeto, Arizona, and Carl began to learn Navajo lore from him. But a deeper knowledge of his own traditional Navajo religion was to come much later in his adulthood.

Rudy was raised a Catholic by his mother, who wanted him to have an understanding of the white man's religion. He was an altar boy for several years. He attended the Catholic school at St. Michael's, disliked it immensely, and his mother sent him to the Presbyterian mission school at Ganado, where he did well. In these same years, when he was with his father, he was taken to Navajo ceremonies and he loved being there. They were always an occasion for him—the songs, the dances, the excitement, and the food.

Wherever they went, the sensitive, impressionable boy saw his father as a brave man, who was tall and powerful and like a movie hero to him. He never forgot the sight of his father, fearless in the presence of danger. One summer day, near Kaibeto at branding time, a vicious bull

Rudy Gorman on right, with Clarence Gorman, his uncle, Chinle, 1934.

49

had been left to the very end. The cowhands had managed to brand him but nobody wanted to untie the rope that held him. Carl Gorman volunteered. He did it swiftly. He raced out of the ring, the bull following him wildly. A horse was standing outside the ring, just beyond the gate. Rudy watched in horror as the bull missed his father by inches and gored the horse. In a second the animal was dead.

The boy carried a drawing pad and pencil with him everywhere. One day he and his father were near a camp where Navajos were dipping sheep. Many families were there. Rudy saw a pretty little girl and wanted to draw her. He asked the child to sit up on a fence and pose for him, like a model. Several times, in a professional tone of voice, he told her to change her position. A white man who worked for the government came over and watched. He turned to Carl Gorman and said, "That boy is terrific. I tell you he's going to be a great artist."

Carl Gorman laughed. It was good to hear the white man say what he himself already believed to be true. He told his Navajo friends what the man had predicted. "That man is a good prophet," he said, and he told his son.

These are moments in a good father-son relationship that are never lost. A child grows into adulthood with a sense of love and a feeling of strength. R. C. remembered these boyhood events as supreme incidents and his father as his hero. He liked to tell the story of the summer at the work camp when the two of them cooked together. Carl would buy a box of soda crackers, a can of pork and beans, orange pop, cookies, potatoes, bacon. He fried the potatoes and the bacon together and poured the hot beans over them, all served in the cracker box. R. C. thought it was the best food there could be. In all the years afterward, he would say it was still his favorite meal.

SEVEN

By the late 1930s Carl Gorman had been working for some time in the government's Stock Reduction Program as an interpreter. The official plan had been instituted to mitigate erosion of the Navajo land from overgrazing. For generations, the flocks of sheep and the herds of cattle and horses owned by the Navajos had been multiplying. It reached the point where the land could no longer support them. The Indian commissioner for the Department of Interior was John Collier, perhaps the most enlightened friend the American Indians had in high office. He instigated a program, with the best of intentions, that was meant to help the Navajo people. Unfortunately, it was to make his name anathema for years to come among the Navajos.

Initial attempts at voluntary stock reduction were made between 1933 and 1935. They were not successful, and the government demanded more reduction. They arranged to purchase 100,000 sheep at $1.00 to $1.50 a head for ewes and $2.25 to $3.00 for wethers (castrated rams) and nonproductive ewes. The mistake was soon obvious. At higher prices, the Navajos sold wethers and the production increased.

By 1937, the reservation was divided into eighteen land management districts. Government range experts set forth the "carrying capacity" of each district. The Navajos were prohibited from moving their stock or themselves from one district to another. There was continuous objection and violation. The maximum size of flocks was set by the government, the capacity calculated in "sheep units." One sheep or one goat equalled one sheep unit, according to how much forage was eaten. One horse equalled five sheep units, one cow four units.

Navajos who had more than the maximum were ordered to reduce their flocks. If they had less than the maximum, they were given permits for what they possessed at the time. Owners who refused to reduce their herds voluntarily were jailed and their livestock slaughtered.

Relentless orders were handed down from officials in the government to the Navajos to reduce livestock—sheep, goats, horses, cattle— all according to government plan. This would stop the land from eroding, they said. The concept seemed simple and logical to the white man. But the Navajos saw it differently. They didn't talk about erosion. The old people said the washes were always there; they could remember them when they were young. The stock reduction program, in addition, failed to take into account the feelings and the heritage of the Navajo people, how much they treasured their animals, and what would happen to the people personally, spiritually, economically. It wasn't simply killing the sheep that had been their livelihood for centuries. It meant killing the sheep they loved and needed. It meant bringing families to the point of starvation. It meant increasing anger at a government that cared nothing for its Indian people.

Under constant pressure, many Navajos were called to meetings in chapter houses to listen to B.I.A. superintendent E. R. Fryer, a lean, stubborn man who admonished them on the need to reduce voluntarily their stock of animals. Carl heard complaints of how the government man would say to them, "Sheep, goats and horses will have to be reduced in numbers, and you people are to say 'yes' and approve the proposal. We don't want you to reject it." The people were told to express how they felt about the stock reduction program, and they would plead to keep their livestock, saying it was their life. But no matter how long the discussions lasted, the reply from Fryer was always a terse statement, "I don't want a 'no' answer. I want a 'yes' answer," until the people finally gave in.

As an interpreter, speaking English, Carl Gorman had to talk out the problems with the government people, and try to explain to them the serious consequences of their orders. As a friend and sympathizer, speaking with his Navajo people, he tried to help them understand why this program of stock reduction was thought to be necessary. If they did not have enough land because of the erosion, he explained to them, how could their sheep, their horses, and their cattle ever have enough land to graze on? A few of the Navajos said they understood. These were primarily the ones who had large ranches and so much livestock they could take the big cut and still survive. Tragically, the same percentage cut applied to those who had small flocks and herds, and these were most of the Navajo people.

Resistance flared across the reservation. Many Navajos were arrested and thrown in jail; their families became destitute. Many were forced to watch their sheep being slaughtered and left in nearby gullies to rot and stink in the burning sunshine.

It was a time of fraud and deception. Carl Gorman boiled with anger when he saw how his people were being cheated by callous white men in charge. The Navajos had been promised a dollar a head or more for each sheep. Most of the time they never got it, before or after the slaughtering. They were also promised $2.50 for each horse that was to be removed from their herd. On one bitter occasion, Carl saw Navajos bring their animals to a designated place near the edge of the reservation. The government officials gave them a dollar a horse, saying take it or leave it. Then the horses were taken across the road beyond the reservation and auctioned off for as much as $30.00 or $40.00 a head.

Despite all his indignation, there was little Carl Gorman felt he could accomplish. He did try to tell the government people that they had to understand about the Navajos, why they resisted so much, why they hated this program even beyond the poverty and the injustices. "You see," he said, imploring them at least to listen, "you have to know something about what our Navajos believe. You have to know that for us our animals have a special, sacred role. They were given to us by our Holy People. The Holy People bring the rain and the grasses that give health to our animals and increase their numbers. Indians only slaughter animals when they need them for food," he said. "Wholesale slaughter is against Indian principle. Our people believe erosion happened in the past because animals were slaughtered needlessly. If there is more reduction, if more animals are slaughtered, sold, taken away, then the Holy People will hold back the rain. The Navajos say that is what really causes the lack of grasses, what brings about the erosion of the land. They believe it is more important to preserve the livestock on the land. Then the rains will come again."

No matter how hard Carl Gorman tried to present the government point of view to his Navajo people, it did no good. How could he argue for a government that forced the reduction on the Navajos in such a cruel way, when it made no sense to them? To the people, there was only the shock of watching their animals die before their eyes.

Into the winter of 1941, Carl Gorman lived with these events, seeing the cold, harsh handling of this program. He was angered that the people of one culture could not come to another with respect, with concern, with a willingness to understand. But he kept on in this discouraging work. He had a family and badly needed the job. He continued to think that perhaps he might do some good.

World War II had been raging in Europe for over two years. Then came the attack on Pearl Harbor on December 7, 1941. The shock waves reached even the far outposts of the Navajo reservation. The radio carried daily reports of the tragic consequences.

Navajo recruits at Fort Wingate, New Mexico; Carl in rear row second from right, 1942.

Carl Gorman was working near Navajo Mountain. He was immediately laid off, along with all the other Indians. The superintendent said they were cutting back on the program because of the war. But the white men were all kept on.

This was the final injustice for Carl Gorman. "If we weren't Indians," he said angrily to his fellow Navajos who had been fired, "we would still be working." He was in bad straits. He had no job or money, and he had no desire to return home. His relations with his wife had continued to deteriorate. Rudy, ten years old by now, had been sent off to a Christian school in Ganado.

Navajos were enlisting in the armed forces. Despite all grievances, many were still willing to come to the defense of their country, just as their fathers had done in World War I. If asked, they said that they were fighting for their own land, protecting the precious Navajo land that they loved.

Carl Gorman enlisted, too. It happened this way, in his words: "We were sitting at Kaibeto, gambling, a bunch of us, when a Navajo boy came over and said he heard over the radio that they wanted thirty Navajo men to volunteer for special duty with the Marines. I said, good, let's join, we'll be better off." He had no noble motives. He was at odds

54

with himself and the world. He was thirty-five years old, and he saw himself as a total failure. He lied about his age in order to be accepted by the Marines. "Maybe I'll get in the thick of the fight real quick," he said to his friends as he left. "And if I get killed, that's all right with me, too." With several others, Carl went to Fort Defiance to sign up with the Marine recruiting team. They took their physical there. They were all passed, signed up, and taken directly to Fort Wingate to be sworn in.

EIGHT

These were the early tragic days after Pearl Harbor, Corregidor, and the series of naval disasters. Not only did the Japanese have superior arms, position, and equipment, they were breaking our tightest communication codes, and the result was death and destruction to the American armed forces.

By the time Carl Gorman had reached the Marine recruiting station at Fort Defiance, a plan had already been developed that would involve him personally in one of the most important secret operations in American military history. It was to be the creation of a military code for combat and invasion purposes that the enemy would never break. And the men destined for this assignment were to be Navajos.

It was a non-Indian, strangely enough, who was presenting the idea responsible for this invulnerable code. He was Philip Johnston, an American engineer who had grown up on the reservation, a missionary's son, who learned to speak Navajo fluently as a child. He had the brilliant, simple concept of using the Navajo language as the basis for a new military code. He knew that it was unbelievably difficult and virtually unknown anywhere else in the world. Johnston excitedly proposed his idea before the Marine top brass at Camp Elliott in California. At first they thought he was insane. He refused to give up. He brought in several Navajos from Los Angeles whom he briefed on how to present a rough code from Navajo to English, and he dramatically proved his case. No cryptography, no code machines. Only a Navajo sender at one end and a Navajo receiver at the other, who translated the message into English and it worked!

The Japanese were already on Guadalcanal in the summer of 1942, breaking all the American codes. From Marine headquarters, a guarded authorization went out for a pilot test group of thirty Navajos to develop the new code. Time was crucial. Recruits had to be found at once who spoke Navajo and English well. They came from the reservation boarding schools and from faraway hogans, too. Most had never gone more than a few score miles from their native homes, and some were so young they forged their age to enlist. All were inducted at Fort Wingate, and Carl Gorman was one of these volunteers. They had no knowledge as yet of the true nature of their mission. All they were told was that they were in special service. There were twenty-nine as they were taken by train through the night to Camp Elliott in California. (One of the selected thirty just never showed up.) Some were light-hearted. Most were filled with trepidation, with a sense of being swept into a fearful unknown. They had been jolted quickly into a harsh, unfamiliar world, from the land and homes in which they had spent their young lives. Carl Gorman understood their silence, their withdrawn behavior. He was twice the age of many of them, some only five or six years older than his own Rudy.

At Camp Elliott these Navajo recruits were assigned to one platoon. They quickly adjusted to what the Americans called "tough training." They had been toughened by the land where they lived, had known extreme heat and cold, extreme hunger and thirst. What was so rough about a basic training hike with an eighty-pound pack on their back, when they thought nothing of walking twenty miles from their hogans to a distant trading post and returning home again with a pack of provisions on their shoulders? They regarded the harshness of training with Navajo humor. "This Marine stuff is nothing," one of them said, laughing, "compared to the hell we had to take in the boarding schools." There was a good deal of prejudice at first. Some of the Marines started off by calling them "Chief" in derision. After the Navajos proved they could take the training, the word became more and more an easy greeting. They had their worst problem with their drill sergeant, a lanky Tennessean with a shrill voice and a manner to match. He was determined to make Marines out of these "lousy Indians." When they kept their hands in their pockets, even for a moment, he filled their pockets with sand and made them drill that way. He cursed them when they changed his "hup-two-three-four" to their own cadence in Navajo. He resented their growing esprit de corps, resented Carl Gorman's growing strength as one of the leaders of the platoon. He did more than push their training. He appeared determined to take out his own personal venom on their darker alien skins. Unexpectedly, he met his match in Carl Gorman.

The Navajo platoon was lined up one morning waiting for their drill sergeant. The moment he arrived he said abruptly, "I'm going to give you clowns a boxing lesson." Moving slowly, officiously down the line of men, he plowed his fist into one Navajo face after the other. The young boys reeled back, some falling from the blow. The tenth man in line was Carl Gorman, who watched the scene with mounting anger. He remembered everything he had learned as an expert boxer in his youth at Albuquerque. He was prepared when his turn came. He skillfully ducked the sergeant's fist. He swiftly hit him with a one-two punch, knocking him flat. The Navajos roared with laughter.

Carl was the hero of the moment. Word of the incident spread rapidly about the camp, even to the CO's office. This act of a raw recruit—an Indian—smashing his fist into the face and the authority of a Marine drill sergeant was unprecedented. The immediate result of such an act could have been a courtmartial and a year in the brig at hard labor, but nothing was done. The drill sergeant made no report. The officers chose to overlook the incident. In view of the circumstance, it was deemed wisest for all concerned to let the matter lie.

There was, in fact, very little prejudice as the Navajos' training went on. There were pep talks, stimulating the boys to think positively beyond their present situation and toward the time when the war would be over. One drill instructor, Sergeant Stephenson, made a strong impression on Carl Gorman. He lectured the men about the importance of having a goal in life and talked to them about determination. "Never say you can't do something," he reiterated. "If someone tells you to move the Statue of Liberty to the West Coast, you don't say how—you say when?"

The excitement and the hard work of drawing up the Navajo code began. The Navajos were to create the code themselves. It was a group effort, all of the men in the original twenty-nine participating with Carl. It was to be a military code that would never be written down, except for training purposes, and then the papers would be destroyed. The training books were locked up every night. The code would be carried over radio or by wire from one talking transmitter to another, and then instantly decoded. The difficult task for the Navajos was to prepare hundreds of key words and military phrases that could be memorized and used efficiently, for urgent communication. Words had to be easily, instantaneously recognized under harsh battle conditions. And there must never be the slightest chance of a mistake.

A whole assortment of military words had to be invented to be used in Navajo. They began with the word for "corps." It became a Navajo word for one of their clans. There was great laughing and yelling as the boys argued for their own family clan name. A division became "salt"; a regiment, "edgewater"; a squad, "black sheep."

It became an exciting game, as they went on to search for the appropriate word. Airplanes became "birds." A bomber was a "buzzard"; a fighter plane, a "hummingbird"; a patrol plane a "crow." Ships became "fish." A battleship was a "whale"; a minesweeper, a "beaver"; a destroyer, a "shark." A route became a "rabbit trail"; a convoy was "moving on water"; a bomb was an "egg."

The alphabet was based on easily remembered words beginning with English letters familiar in the Navajo culture. *A* was for "ant" ("woll-a-chee"). *J* was for "jackass" ("tkele-cho-gi"), *S* for "sheep" ("dibeh"), *Y* for "yucca" ("tsah-as-zih").

This was a fantastic requirement that was demanded of the Navajo boys: to memorize so much in the urgent timetable of only a few weeks, the hundreds of words and phrases, most of them foreign to their own basic culture. But it was a feat that Carl Gorman knew would not be insurmountable. He tried to explain why to the communications officer, who was amazed at the speed with which the Navajo boys were drilling. "You have to understand," Carl Gorman said, "that for us, everything is memory. You see, Lieutenant, it's part of our heritage. We have no written language. Our songs, our prayers, our stories, they're all handed down from grandfather to father to children—and we listen, we hear, we learn to remember everything. It's part of our training."

The Navajos, caught up in the excitement of building their code, began testing each other, message after message, in terse Marine Corps instructions: "Machine gun fire on left flank . . . ," "Platoon 4 to dig in. Losses running high. . . ." "Change coordinates, numbers as follows. . . ." In a testing demonstration before the military staff, they astounded the officers with the speed of their communications. With two Navajos separated at a considerable distance, Carl Gorman behind one barracks wall and his friend Bill McCabe behind another, a six-line coded message was completed in exactly two minutes; it was sent to a receiver in Navajo and delivered back in English!

"It goes in, in Navajo? And it comes out in English?" an officer exclaimed. "Dammit, how does it work?" he thundered at Carl Gorman.

"It's very simple, sir," Carl said to him. "It's because that is the damnedest talking code machine over there where my Navajo friend McCabe is and I'm a talking code machine over here."

From that day on the term *Code Talkers* stayed with the Navajos. Three of the Navy's best-trained intelligence experts were brought in to test their messages, intercepting them, attempting to break them down. They failed completely, detecting no basic pattern. The new code seemed foolproof. It was ready for testing under combat conditions.

The Navajo Code Talkers were ordered to the South Pacific, assigned to the First and Second Marine Corps Division. Two of the men, John Benally, and Johnny Manuelito, whose records had been outstanding, received orders to remain behind as future instructors. A request for the training of hundreds more Navajo Code Talkers was already at Marine Corps Headquarters in Washington. The implementation would

Code Talker Carl Gorman at observation post on Saipan, June 27, 1944.

depend entirely on the success of the small pilot group now going into the South Pacific.

By the fall of 1942, the Japanese were sweeping over Guadalcanal. They infiltrated Marine forces, cutting down their patrols, breaking every code. Heading toward this scene of chaos and fierce fighting was a small band of Code Talkers. Thirteen of them, including Carl in the Sixth Marine Regiment of the Second Division, came from their staging area in New Zealand. As their convoy approached Guadalcanal, they were practicing their Navajo code. Instant bedlam broke out on the island. Marine radio operators kept screaming wildly, "Get those Japs off our frequencies!" Dawn broke on Guadalcanal before the knowledge finally seeped through that these were their own men, Marines with a strange new code operating.

The Code Talkers were with the first landing parties. They moved at once into every phase of key action. Working with Carl Gorman all the way were his friends William Yazzie, Jack Nez, and Oscar Ilthma. The Code Talkers were with the jungle patrols, behind enemy lines, on hilltops spotting artillery range. The calls began to go out for them, for help, for support. They were proving themselves in action.

The Japanese were bewildered by the new code—and completely frustrated. Their highly trained intelligence experts, some of them graduates of American universities, could no longer break down the makeshift combat codes, pig Latin messages, urgent dispatches in U.S. baseball lingo. Their radio men, in desperation, tried to jam the Code Talkers' frequencies. But these were changed on them immediately.

On Guadalcanal, Carl Gorman began to look at himself clearly for the first time. His sense of pride in his personal achievement as a Marine grew stronger each day. One night a Marine sergeant who had become his friend started to ask him questions about his life back home. "Hey, Gorman, what's your religion? What's it like?"

"Me? I'm Presbyterian," Carl Gorman answered. It was an old response, the way he had been brought up to speak of his religion by his mother.

"A Presbyterian? You're crazy, Gorman!" the sergeant laughed. "That's a white man's religion. I want to know about your Indian religion. Are you trying to be white, Gorman? You'll never make it! Your head's still flat in the back!"

The blunt harangue brought a new insight to Carl Gorman. "I realized I was an Indian," he said. "The Marine Corps opened my eyes. I realized I had a culture, all the things the white people have." Why was there need for any pretense? He was a Navajo. He came from the land of the Navajos. He was here with his fellow Navajos. They were doing a job they could be proud of as Navajos. He, Carl Gorman, who had been beaten and chained in school for speaking Navajo, was now being of service to his country and helping save the lives of his fellow Marines by speaking Navajo, by talking their code in Navajo.

Carl was beginning to be aware that wherever he went, he could walk with pride and with strength. He drew a new sense of satisfaction in watching some of his Navajo friends pray at dawn, taking corn pollen from the pouches that they carried at their waist. They performed the ritual by offering the pollen to the cardinal directions, east, south, west, and north in an upward movement toward the sky; then they touched the pollen to the tongue and then to the crown of the head, again facing east. A man's spirit would breathe through its essence as he spoke his prayers, ending in "It is finished in beauty. . . . It is finished in beauty."

As the battle for Guadalcanal approached its climax, the Code Talkers were being called upon incessantly. A vast Japanese fleet loaded with fresh troops was moving up the Coral Sea. Their submarines landed special fighting units ashore. One Navajo Code Talker volunteered to climb to the highest ridge, past enemy snipers, to spot and position the subs. He outwitted the Japanese who were trying frantically to find him, to block his message. Witnessing the great sea battle, he reported in Navajo the first flight of enemy vessels. The young Code Talker, at headquarters receiving his message, translated exultantly to the general and staff about him, "We've beaten them! They're running away!"

For all the Marines, it was the end of their first great task in the South Pacific. For the Code Talkers, it was proof of their worth under fire. Their code was still unbroken. Their success would spur Marine Headquarters to order the training of hundreds more who would be assigned throughout the Pacific. Their destiny would take many of them far ahead to the ultimate triumphant test at Iwo Jima.

Except for brief respites, for rest and retraining at New Zealand or Australia, the next two years became a time of invasions, of death and nightmares for the Marines, for the Code Talkers, and for Carl Gorman. With each landing, always under terrible fire, he never believed that he would survive. He did, and went on to the next. He saw several of his friends die in the fierce fight at Tarawa as they performed their duty. He had no fear of death himself. But now he had a deep desire to survive, to find a way of life in the future that would give him the sense of dignity and self-respect he found in the Marines. He had been weakened by malaria, but he continued to fight. After the successful invasion of Saipan in 1944, he was laid low by the tropical disease and hospitalized. He was there when he heard the daily reports of the invasion of Iwo Jima. He knew the vital role that the Code Talkers had been asked to perform during that invasion. They transmitted key messages from ship to shore, to combat patrols, to planes in the sky, to artillery fire. When Mount Surabachi was taken, the triumphant announcement of victory was radioed in Navajo from Code Talker to Code Talker throughout the South Pacific. Afterwards, Marine officers stated that the invasion of Iwo Jima could not have been accomplished without the Navajo Code Talkers. They were in the midst of it, from start to finish. They manned the radio aboard ship. They were with the landing craft, going ashore with the first wave of Marines onto the murderous volcanic beaches. They continued to send their messages while bombs were landing all around them, giving vital information to command officers, where to pinpoint enemy location, where to send men and rockets. Their achievement was heroic.

By the end of the war, eight Code Talkers had died in action in the South Pacific. As for the rest, when they returned from the war, they had new feelings about themselves. They had traveled ten thousand miles from their Navajo homeland. They had helped defeat a powerful enemy and had been treated with respect by their fellow Marines. Now they could walk with their heads up. They had done more than survive. They had proved themselves. Many felt they could go anywhere and not be afraid. A good number returned to the reservation and began to

Carl on furlough with his father, on a trip to
Flagstaff, Arizona, 1945.

work themselves up into positions of leadership among their own people.
Many went into the cities, to try their fortunes in a new world, in a
new way.

Carl Gorman was evacuated from Saipan for continued medical
treatment. He spent two months in Pearl Harbor in a naval hospital and
finally was sent to a Marine Corps rehabilitation center in Klamath
Falls, Oregon. In the long days of rest and recuperation, he began to
draw again. During the time of war, Carl had managed somehow to find
moments to sketch—faces and bodies of men in action, a Marine doing
guard duty, silhouetted against the dawn. He packed them away in his
sea bag, along with mementos he had collected from Guadalcanal to
Tarawa, but when he was sent back to this country the bag was lost.
Months later, it arrived at the rehabilitation hospital. All the mementos
were gone—the beautiful collection of seashells he had picked up, odd-
shaped pieces of coral, stray enemy bullets. But most tragic of all, for
Carl, his drawings were gone too.

A psychiatrist at the hospital helped alter the direction of Carl
Gorman's life. A compassionate human being, concerned with the men-

tal condition of the men who had returned from war, he talked with them at length about the ordeals they had been through—the death of comrades, the terrors of invasion, the nightmares. He talked with Carl often, long, leisurely heartfelt discussions. He asked Carl what he was going to do when let out from service. "Perhaps we can help you," he said. "What are your plans? What are you going to do with your life now, Gorman?" At that moment, passing through Carl's mind, were all the drawings he had loved to do as a child, in school, and the last ones in the Marine Corps.

"I think I'd like to go to art school," Carl said. "I've always been interested in drawing. I've never had a chance." He pulled out a folder of his recent drawings from a table beside his bed. The psychiatrist was impressed; the sketches were sensitive and compelling. Carl ought to go to art school, he said. Under the G.I. Bill, he would have four years coming to him. The government would pay his way, and Carl could select any school he wanted.

Late in 1944, Carl was given leave to go back to the Navajo reservation on a two-week furlough. He visited his father's home first and learned there that his wife, Adelle, had been living with another man for several years. During his duty overseas, an allotment had been always taken out of Carl's pay for the support of his family. Certain now that his marriage with Adelle was over, for both of them, Carl went to see Judge John Curley at Fort Defiance. He told him the entire story, and the judge granted him a divorce.

NINE

In the winter of 1945, Carl Gorman received his honorable discharge from the Marine Corps at Barstow, California. He had no intention of returning to the reservation. Instead, he got a job working at the Marine Corps Supply Base in the maintenance and painting crew. He wrote away immediately to a list of top art schools, including the Rhode Island School of Design and the Chicago Art Institute, seeking out the best.

In charge of property and supply at the base was a tall, lean, middle-aged New Englander, Clifford Wilson. He knew Navajos well, liked and respected them. The base was one of the main places that hired Navajos, and they had an excellent work record. Carl Gorman went over to Wilson's office one morning to get some tools. They started talking. Over a period of time they got to know each other and had a good rapport. Wilson was disturbed when Carl, who was a good worker, came to tell him that he had been fired by his foreman on the paint job where he was employed. After talking the whole situation over with Carl, Wilson was sure there was some misunderstanding on the part of the foreman. He went directly to the colonel of the base, explained what had happened, and as a result of his intervention, Carl Gorman was reinstated.

When Wilson invited his Navajo friend to a Sunday dinner, Carl met his daughter, Mary, for the first time. She was tall, blonde, interested in art. They were immediately drawn to each other.

Mary Excie Wilson was born on September 4, 1924, in Warren, Rhode Island, the only child of Clifford and Mary Wilson. Her father adored her, and there was never enough he could do for her, especially during her high school years when she suffered continually from severe sinus

Carl in Barstow, California, 1946.

infections. He gave up his job as paymaster for U.S. Rubber Co. in Providence and moved the family out to Tucson in the Arizona desert, where the hot, dry climate helped Mary's health. Here she studied art over a period of two years.

Wilson got work during the war with the Southern Pacific Railroad. He left this job to go into tungsten mining and moved his family to Globe, Arizona, where the Pinto mining company, of which he was part owner, had claims in the nearby Superstition Mountains. But the war was coming to an end, and the government was no longer stockpiling tungsten. Wilson went to work for the Santa Fe Railroad as a relief timekeeper. Within a year, he moved his family to many stations along the railroad—to Prescott and Williams in Arizona, to Gallup in New Mexico and to Amboy, Newberry, and Mojave in California. They lived in a railroad car for three months. It was a trying time for Mary and her mother, but an interesting experience, too. Most of the workers on the tracks were Navajos. Coming in contact with them in so many places, Mary had the opportunity to know them. She felt comfortable, in tune with them. When the family reached Barstow and Wilson went to work as a civilian at the Marine Corps base, the family was finally able to settle down. They lived on the base in a civilian apartment.

When Mary met Carl Gorman in February 1946, he was in his late thirties, extremely handsome and youthful. The fact that Carl was an Indian made him all the more attractive. She could remember how her father had always spoken sympathetically about Indians, how he used to read her stories about Indians when she was a child, always encour-

68

aging her to think of Indians as decent people, as human beings whom she should respect. He had once written a story himself that told of the coming of the Vikings to North America and of the love affair between a beautiful Norse girl, the daughter of the sea captain, and a young Indian brave.

When Mary and Carl had known each other awhile, she told him of a vivid dream she had had. It was about Navajos, she said. Mary had been working part-time in the Barstow library. The woman librarian there did not hide the fact that she was strongly prejudiced against the Navajo workers. She ordered Mary not to give library cards to any of them who wanted to borrow books. "They're just transients," she said. "They'll steal everything—they're not to be trusted." The woman's words infuriated Mary but she kept still. She knew in her own mind what she would do.

One day when Mary was substituting for the librarian, two young Navajos came in. One of them asked for a book about the Navajos, *Children of the People,* by Dorothea Leighton. Mary gave him a card, and he checked out the book. She was away from the library a week and she worried about the Navajo man, what would happen if he didn't return the book. "This is the dream I had," she said to Carl. "I was back in the library, and I walked to the cart, where returned books were placed. And there, high up on the second shelf, about three books from the right,

Mary Excie Wilson in front of Barstow Public Library, 1948.

was the Leighton book!" Then she added, "Two days later I was going into town from the base and I went right to the library. I checked the cart and I felt an enormous relief. There was the book, in exactly the same place I had dreamed it would be."

"I like the way the story ends," Carl Gorman said. "You dream like a true Navajo."

The truth was that Mary felt like a Navajo. When Carl talked to her about Navajo ways, about the concept of "living in harmony with nature," he didn't have to explain what he meant. She understood, she said, for intuitively, she had felt that way for a long, long time.

Carl Gorman's enrollment at Otis Art Institute in Los Angeles took place in the fall of 1947. He had not yet heard from the schools in the East. Coming to Los Angeles from Barstow one Saturday afternoon, he gravitated toward the Ritz Bar on Main Street, a spot where Indians from different tribes congregated. He got into a conversation with a Navajo named Ralph Roanhorse, who took pride in being an artist and said he had studied at the Otis Art Institute. What was Carl doing, he asked, trying to get into schools thousands of miles away? Why didn't he go to Otis? It was becoming one of the best on the entire West Coast.

Carl followed Ralph Roanhorse's advice and went to see the dean at Otis Art Institute. Within a month he was admitted. The G.I. Bill paid his tuition and gave him seventy-five dollars a month to live on. He found a room in a cheap hotel within walking distance of the school. He learned to eat spaghetti day in and day out at a cost of twenty-five cents a meal. To supplement his income, he found work at a jewelry store on Olvera Street in downtown Los Angeles near the Old Plaza. The owner was a short, round, bejeweled lady, who spent most of her time sitting in meditation at the rear of the store. People who came into the store rarely saw her. She had so much jewelry on her from neck to waist that she looked like a display, Carl said. Only her eyes moved.

From the day of his enrollment at Otis, Carl was part of a whole new world of personal adventure and progress, a world that he had always longed to be in. All about him were enthusiastic students. There were men and women of all types, many of them ex-G.I.'s with one purpose in mind: a career in art.

At first, Carl was allowed freedom at Otis to do as he pleased, to work in whatever way he chose. As he would say later, with a wry smile, he thought that all he had to do to be an artist was to get paint, brushes, and canvas, and paint away. So he proceeded to do this. An instructor observed Carl at work. After a short time he approached Carl and was very direct. "You've been trying to build a house," he said, "the windows going in first. But there are no foundations." Then he added, "If I were you I'd put the paint and brushes away."

The instructor proceeded to outline what he considered an intelli-

Carl in front of Otis Art Institute, Los Angeles, 1950.

gent course of study, if Carl truly wanted to be an artist. He suggested first a composition class, then a design class, followed by a color class. These three things had to be learned from the beginning, he said, and had to be learned well. The words sank into Carl's consciousness, never to be forgotten: composition, design, color. These were his studies for the whole first year.

In his second year, Carl went on to a course in life study and anatomy, drawing from live models. Discovering how important it was to know the bones and muscles of the human figure, he learned to draw them with facility.

In his third year at Otis, Carl finally began to study painting. His instructor, Joseph Mugnaini, was an Italian who loved to listen to Grand Opera as he painted. Carl came to see him in his studio on the first day. Hearing the music, he spread his arms wide and burst out singing. The memories of his childhood, of his mother, of his love for drawing while listening to opera himself, all came rushing back.

He told the instructor all about it, the records he used to listen to, the great singers of the past. The two men instantly became good friends. They would listen to music together and paint while they listened. Through the rest of his life, whenever he started to work in his studio, drawing or painting, Carl would put on an opera record. He liked to say that it gave him inspiration, made him feel good, put him in the mood.

Carl worked in different media, including oils, watercolor, and casein. In his fourth year, he studied sculpture and worked in ceramics. And he painted continually, never forgetting to judge his own works in terms of composiiton, design, color.

A distinguished group of artists was on the faculty at Otis. Carl was exposed to the teaching of all of them: Mugnaini, in painting; Ejnar Hansen, advanced figure painting; Leonard Herbert, drawing; Richard Flu and Gaylord Richmond, life drawing; Wayne Long, sculpture, ceramics; Boris Deutsch, oil painting.

A wide world of art was opening up to Carl Gorman now. He came to it with the enthusiasm of a student who loved his work, avidly absorbing instruction and knowlege. He wanted to try everything, to experiment in all forms of media and methods. His goal was to grow in his art, to be free, to be bold, and to excel. He went back to the masters of the past, continually studying their work. He fell in love with Rembrandt. He became a devotee of Michelangelo, endlessly copying the structure of his figures, the bones, the torsos, arms, legs, muscles.

His son Rudy was still in high school in Ganado, and he came several times to see his father in Los Angeles. Brimming with enthusiasm, Carl would talk to his son about all the exciting things he was learning. As he talked, he became the teacher, exploring the concepts of color and space, shades of light, and rhythm in painting; he expounded on art history and his love for masters. It was as if he was trying to impart all that he himself was learning at Otis to his own sensitive son. He dwelled at great length on Rembrandt, and Rudy was to come to admire Rembrandt as much as his father did.

What was most important to Carl Gorman was that he was learning to be an artist—not just willing to imitate others but to express ideas and feelings, in his own way, as strongly as he could. In these four years he had come to know that there were many different ways of painting, different methods, styles, techniques. During the war he had seen a wide world of action and of people. Now he wanted to observe and record this new environment and its people.

He took breaks from the rigorous day-and-night schedule he followed to go to professional hockey games at the Los Angeles Arena. With sketch pad and pencil along, he would draw pictures of the helmeted hockey players in action as they raced down the ice, blocking, crouching. He drew a goal tender with stick outstretched to ward off a flying puck, vibrant, powerful figures swiftly outlined on paper. On warm weekends he would to go Santa Monica and draw the people there on the beach. The human figure, in all its varied and antic display, fascinated him as did all aspects of the white man's world. When the San Francisco Opera came to the Shrine Auditorium in Los Angeles on its annual tour, he would go as often as he could afford the price of the cheapest seat. *La Bohème* became his favorite, taking precedence over his first love, *La Traviata.*

More conscious of his feelings as an Indian, he was keenly aware of the problems of other Indians who had come to Los Angeles after the war, seeking a new life, hoping to find jobs, money, and ordinary comforts away from the rigors of the reservation existence. Most were finding that their hopes would be denied, replaced only too often with rejection and prejudice.

He became active in the Indian Center located on Beverly Boulevard in Los Angeles. By 1948, while still a student at Otis, he was chairman of the Indian Arts and Crafts show sponsored by the center.

As a veteran who was fortunate enough to be making his way in Anglo society, Carl was angry at the treatment other returning Indian veterans were receiving. Coming back from a trip to Arizona, where the state law still prohibited Indians from drinking, he expressed his resentment in a crude but powerful oil painting of a barroom scene. An Indian soldier on crutches in G.I. uniform is standing painfully with his back to the open door. A gross bartender and three chunky bald-headed men sitting on bar stools, eyes glaring, are pointing long white fingers like guns at the veteran. On the mirror, directly behind them, in harsh relief, is a sign with a picture of an Indian, which says "Not Allowed."

In 1951, after four years at Otis Art Institute, the provisions of Carl's G.I. Bill ran out. With excellent endorsements from the dean of the school and from his instructors, he got a position that same year at Douglas Aircraft in Santa Monica as a technical illustrator. It not only paid him a good salary, with long-range benefits, but it gave him a newfound sense of security. He was also intrigued by the work. He enrolled in a course in blueprint reading at Santa Monica Technical School, which helped him in his work in which he took complicated mechanical or scientific concepts that were handed to him and drew them in strongly delineated shapes and forms. Draftsmen made blueprints of a project, of plane components or parts of a missile system, and Carl rendered them in three-dimensional drawings so that the executives could visualize what their engineers were talking about.

Carl enjoyed the new milieu of the aircraft plant, the camaraderie of the men and women working there. As at Otis, he was fortunate that he found comparatively little prejudice against him as an Indian. Perhaps it was because he commanded respect, both in his appearance and in his serious attitude toward his obligations. Perhaps it was his prevailing good humor, which surprised many of his Anglo companions who had a stereotype in mind of the stoic, grim-faced Indian.

Now that he had money to pay his own way, Carl went back to Otis Art Institute, three nights a week, three hours a night. He continued primarily with painting and life drawing. He researched diligently the different techniques of his art. A friend at Douglas, intrigued by his seriousness, asked Carl when he would be finished with all this studying. "I'll tell you what Michelangelo said," Carl replied. "When someone asked him the same question, he just said, 'Art is a lifetime study.'"

Indian themes began to appear in his work. Carl was determined that if he was going to be an artist, he was going to make it as a Navajo and an Indian in a white man's world. He was going to be himself. He had learned that lesson of identity well, in the war. As the years went on, he was more determined than ever not to be caught between two worlds, as so many Indians had been, never sure of themselves, filled with their own doubts, victims of prejudice. That was no good, he said. You have to stay proud of yourself, stand on your own feet as an Indian. But how could you be proud, if you're ignorant of your Indian heritage? Or even worse, if you denied it?

Seeking inspiration from his culture, Carl remembered scenes and stories from his childhood. He painted ancient ruins, the oft-told Navajo myths, a squaw dance, riders on horseback. He wanted his paintings to come alive, communicate emotionally to the viewer. "Why don't you paint the way the other Indians do?" an instructor asked him. "I don't paint for the public at large," Carl replied angrily. "I paint what I want to, and the way I want to! It's part of my life. I want to express on canvas the history of the Navajos—where they came from, where they are going."

By 1954, after three years of night study at Otis, "moonlighting in art," he called it, Carl felt sure enough of himself and of his skills to be on his own. While still working at Douglas, he continued to paint and explore all media. He experimented with painting in the very old art of encaustic, where the brush is dipped into a bowl of hot wax and then into a bowl of color; when the mixture on the brush is applied to the canvas, it is said to burn-in and last forever. He strove to capture the vitality and the excitement of the old Navajo legends. He painted Navajo Yei-bi-chei dances and Apache Ghan dances on ceramic tiles with ceramic paint that had to be fired many times. He designed textiles, his Indian motifs showing a fresh abstract quality on the fabric.

He never lost his love for the horses he used to draw on scraps of paper when he was a child. His memory would go back to the periods he spent on his father's ranch. He began to paint horses in different media—in oil and watercolor.

At this time, Carl chose to sign his Indian name on his works, Kin-ya-onny beyeh, "Son of Towering House People." He found satisfaction in the process of expressing his feelings on canvas, of putting these things down, so people would understand what he wanted to say. "I enjoy the fact that somebody likes my work," he said. "It means they appreciate the way I express myself in art. It makes me feel as though they're part of me."

In these developing years, he exhibited at the Navajo Tribal Fair, and at the New Mexico State Fair in Albuquerque. He showed annually at the Douglas Employees' Exhibit in Santa Monica, at the Otis Art

74

Carl's favorite picture of Mary,
Mojave Desert, California, 1950.

Institute Alumni Association shows, and also at the Indian Center in
Los Angeles. It was here that Lowell Butler, art editor of *Westways,* the
official magazine of the Automobile Club of Southern California, saw
his work. He was captured by the strength of it and commissioned Carl
to do a cover for his magazine.

In 1955, the Gallup Public Library held a one-man show of Carl
Gorman's work. The head librarian, Octavia Felin, had maintained a
policy of encouraging artists, and the library had housed many art exhibits. She said of Carl, "He showed high development as an Indian
artist who could really grasp non-Indian style."

Nine years passed since Carl and Mary first met in Barstow. During
a great part of that time, Carl was almost totally absorbed in his art
career. Mary worked on the Marine base in the payroll department.
About once a month, Carl took the long trip to Barstow to visit his
brother Steve, who was working there, and to be with Mary. Several
summers he went back to his old job in maintenance at the Marine

Corps base. Mary's parents had bought a home in town, and Carl came to see her there. He gave her instructions in oil painting in the family kitchen. Evenings, they sat in the living room and talked about art. When he was in Los Angeles, they exchanged letters every few weeks. They wrote about their work, the things they did, the people they saw. They never wrote about love or their feelings about each other. There was never a word about their future together or about marriage. They had a good friendship going, Carl thought.

In all this time, Carl went back to the reservation only three times, primarily to see his father. The reunion was always warm. After the death of his wife Alice, Nelson Gorman had married a young Navajo girl from the region of Black Mesa. The big house in Chinle still felt empty and strange to Carl without his mother, even though she had been dead for more than twenty years. Memories of what had been came back to haunt him. Each time he quickly returned to Los Angeles.

This was a period of security for Carl. His art career was going well. His pay at Douglas was good, and he was putting money in the bank. He began to write to Mary and to phone her almost every Sunday morning. Mary could sense a strange new attitude on the part of her father, the beginning of a hostility toward Carl whenever he came to visit her. She thought it was only jealousy at first. Sunday mornings, when her father wanted to go off with the family, he resented it when Mary said she had to wait for Carl's call. The closer their relationship grew, the more hostile her father became. Her father's change of feelings troubled Mary. It hurt her deeply to see him upset whenever she and Carl were together. He interrogated her about their relationship, asked questions about Carl's Indian wife, and Mary explained that Carl and his wife had been divorced soon after he came out of the Marines. Wilson never came to the point of forbidding his daughter to be with Carl, a Navajo. But he invariably left her with the feeling that he thought she was making a terrible mistake.

In 1956, matters came to a head. An open break took place between Mary and her father, when Carl sent her a record album, his beloved opera, *La Traviata.* Her father became furious. He refused to let her play "those records," because Carl had given them to her. Mary immediately made a decision about herself and Carl. She felt so much a part of his life now, was so proud of him and his work, had always been so drawn to him, it didn't make sense for them to be apart any longer. She was determined to go her own way, and her father would have to live with that decision. It was then that Mary wrote the letter in which she proposed to Carl. She felt it no longer mattered what her parents wanted. There was something between her and Carl that was deeper, more important than any of them.

Carl had thought of being married to Mary before this time, but he had never said anything about it. He worried about the problem of prejudice. He felt he could cope with it, but he worried about its effect on Mary. By now he knew the way her father felt toward him, an Indian, who was close to his daughter. Other people might feel the same way, too, if they were married. When he got her letter, he came at once to Barstow and they talked. They put aside all their fears and decided to get a marriage license.

Despite her father's vehement objections, Carl and Mary were married in the Church of the Valley, in Apple Valley, California, March 24, 1956. Carl's brother Steve and his wife Eloise stood up with them as best man and matron of honor. Also present were several friends. Mary's parents stayed away.

After the ceremony, they went back to Barstow with Steve and Eloise, and they loaded all of Mary's things into Carl's station wagon, a green Chevy with wood panels. They set off for Los Angeles. Halfway there, they had a flat tire. It was long past midnight before they reached the guesthouse behind a big home in Sherman Oaks where Carl lived. The driveway was lined with orange trees in blossom, and the mockingbirds kept them awake the rest of the night.

They lived in the crowded guesthouse for only a few months. When Mary became pregnant, they bought a small home in Encino, a few miles to the west in the San Fernando Valley. Carl had his studio in the garage where he could work nights and weekends, listening to his opera music for inspiration.

Mary's parents remained in Barstow. In a whole year, they visited her on only one weekend, bringing her some of her belongings. They came when they knew Carl would be at work at Douglas. Mary and Carl's first child, a son, Alfred Kee, was born in April 1957. His birth brought the family all together; in Barstow, Mary's father gave out cigars grandly to everyone. When the parents came to Encino to visit the new grandchild, they brought Mary her father's long, embroidered baby dress, and they took a picture of Kee in it. Clifford Wilson had been seriously ill for some time without telling Mary. He saw her and Kee on only a few more occasions. He was to die of cancer in July 1958.

"I liked him," Carl said to Mary after the funeral of her father. "It was too bad we didn't get together earlier. We could have been a good, close family." He felt compassion for the man who had befriended him and then turned against him. What a waste of precious time, he thought, wishing only that the older man could have accepted their love. Mary's mother came to live with them after her husband's death. Like many Navajos in today's world, Carl had long disregarded the taboo of avoiding one's mother-in-law, and he and Mary often joked about her presence. In fact, she helped them finance a larger home in Northridge, a few miles farther out in the valley.

Mary was continually supportive of Carl's artwork. She refused to let him get discouraged; she kept reminding him of his splendid talent. One night, she was outside the house in Northridge while he was working in his studio. She saw a painting of Carl's sticking out of the trash can, one he had thrown away. She brought it to him. He shrugged. He told her he sometimes got disgusted with things he painted and just wanted to get rid of them, throw them away, start all over, perhaps the next day do something better.

But this one was powerful, Mary said. She saw strength in the painting, a sheer thrust of lightning on the mesa. People would admire this, she said. Carl listened to her. He later said that he would never have succeeded without her.

From the time of their marriage, Carl's career went into high gear. In August 1956, the cover commissioned by the editor of *Westways* magazine was finished. It would be seen by hundreds of thousands of the Automobile Club's members. Carl had chosen as the subject for his painting a part of the Enemy Way Ceremony and had titled it *Navajo War Dance*. Set against the soaring background of Round Rock, near Chinle, two groups of Navajo men heavily robed are trying to outsing each other. A note to Carl from Lowell Butler, the editor, read: "Here are some proofs of your cover. Congratulations! It is terrific!"

In the fall of 1956, Mary went with Carl, as his bride, on her first trip into the Navajo country. She visited Carl's father and her new relatives in Chinle. That same year, the Gallup Indian Center featured the work of "the famous Indian painter, Carl Gorman"; included was the outstanding *Aborigines*, a powerful portrait of Indian faces. At the Navajo Tribal Fair, Carl took first prize for his *Navajo Medicine Man*, a large painting of a medicine man on horseback driving away a band of sheep given to him as payment for his services.

When the annual Navajo Fair was due to open in 1959, Carl could not leave his job at Douglas Aircraft. He was at work as a technical illustrator on a tight security missile program. Mary felt it was important that he keep on showing at the Navajo Fair. She insisted on going to set up the booth on the opening day. That was the time when the art dealers and traders came to make their selections. Carl's younger brother, Steve, and his wife, Eloise, went with her.

Early September is often a time for thunderstorms in the Southwest. The three arrived at the fairgrounds in Window Rock in a drenching rain. Hundreds of Navajo families were already there, having come from all parts of the reservation. The wagons and horses and a scattering of autos and pickup trucks were filling the open parking area by the highway, away from the reviewing stand. Many had pitched their tents there. Children and dogs were everywhere. Mary and her relatives set up their own tent in the pelting rains. This would be their accommodations for three nights.

The fair opened on Wednesday, the day the buyers came to select the best of the arts and crafts brought by the Indians. Food stands were set up where people could buy bread, melons, chile, and roast corn. On Thursday, the Gallup Lion's Club arranged a huge barbecue, served free to all Navajos—barbecued beef, beans and bread, watermelon, ice cream, and coffee. The people ate anywhere, some squatting on the ground, some on benches, some in their cars. They formed a colorful assembly, the men in their broad-brimmed hats and bright shirts girded with heavy silver concho belts, the women, in their velvet blouses and gathered calico skirts, all wearing their beautiful bracelets and necklaces of silver and turquoise. It was a time of reunion for old friends, for families that hadn't seen each other since the last fair. It was a time for politicians to come out and talk, and no one listened.

Mary hung Carl's paintings for display in the rude wooden booth that had been assigned to her. She sold several of them before the day was over. The very first one, which delighted her the most, was the painting she had rescued several years before from the ashcan after Carl had thrown it away. Paul F. Huldermann, a prominent Scottsdale art dealer, bought it. He had high praise for the painting, and he told Mary that he had faith in Carl's future.

By the late 1950s, Carl had won over fifty awards for his paintings. He showed in many places in California—in Santa Monica, Riverside, Los Angeles, San Francisco. His reputation continued to grow as reviews and press notices appeared. One local critic seemed overwhelmed by the newness and vitality of his Indian art. After a Northridge, California exhibit in November 1960, the reviewer, Kenneth Bromfield, wrote: "Studying his work was, for me, an emotional, roaming orgy. Gorman is one of the pioneers of a new and striking trend in American Indian painting; incredibly fearless and flamboyant in his use of color. His paintings dance, writhe and grip with the searing reality of the Arizona desert; his characters are living, feeling people."

The director of the Southwest Museum in Los Angeles, Carl S. Dentzel, viewed the same exhibit and bought the prize-winning water-color, *The Round-up*, for his museum's collection.

In striking contrast to the awards and praise, there was a bitter fact of life in the Indian art world that Carl had to face. When he showed in California, no gallery was closed to him because he was an Indian, or because he painted in a specific style. His work was judged on its own merit. But in the Southwest, the conditions were totally different. There was segregation of Indian artists. The only shows that were open to them were the Indian shows. Once their work was exhibited, they would be invited back. It was their only path to recognition.

From the Mississippi River west, the three main Indian art shows for Southwest artists were housed in the Philbrook Art Center in Tulsa, Oklahoma; the Gallup, New Mexico Inter-Tribal Indian Ceremonial; and the American Indian Annual at the Fine Arts Museum in Santa Fe. The big art traders and dealers, whose influence dominated these prestigious exhibits of the Southwest and who were primarily responsible for building the reputation of an Indian artist, stayed with the traditional—the flat, decorative, two-dimensional style that characterized Indian painting. It sold readily for them at higher and higher prices, and they resisted the introduction of new techniques or new styles.

Most of the successful Indian paintings in the 1940s and 1950s followed the precepts set down by the School of Indian Painting founded by Dorothy Dunn in Santa Fe in 1932. She encouraged the use of water-based media and the flat calligraphic approach. It was a conservative style, not far removed from that used by the Pueblo Indians for their wall paintings and by the Plains Indians in their decorative art. Working later in this traditional mode, highly successful artists like Beatien Yazz and Andy Tsinajinie achieved outstanding results with their sensitive paintings.

When Carl Gorman studied at Otis in the late 1940s and early 1950s, a new world was opening up to him. He chose not to paint in the flat, illustrative style that characterized Indian painting at the time. He resented being told that as an Indian he must work in the strict, traditional manner. Into the early 1960s, even as he was becoming more successful on the West Coast, his paintings were not regarded as that of a genuine Indian artist by the big shows of the Southwest. They maintained that Carl had broken with the rules and refused to paint in the accepted style. Theirs were competitive shows, and the artist's work had to fit into their strict traditional competitive categories. Carl could exhibit at the Navajo Tribal Fair in Window Rock, Arizona; the only requirement was that the submitting artist be a Navajo.

The time for a breakthrough, however, was at hand, and it came about in the town of Scottsdale, near the growing community of Phoenix. Its focal point was the first Scottsdale National Indian Art Exhibit in 1962. The sponsor and chief coordinator was Paul F. Huldermann, whose House of Six Directions had become a center for Indian arts and crafts of the region. For some time now Indian painters and craftsmen, like Charles Loloma, Lloyd Kiva, Kenneth Begay, and Bahah-Zhonie had found no barriers here to their creativity. "Here," wrote Huldermann later, "there were no unsurpassable hurdles for the artist to make himself understood and heard. Here in Scottsdale there was no separation between him and his white fellow man, his friends, or his customers if you will."

No one was told what to make or how to paint. Artists were not asked to repeat themselves, but rather encouraged to be distinctive and creative in their work. They searched to express themselves in ways not yet tried. "The origin of the Scottsdale National," wrote Huldermann,

> was as a test, you might say, to feel the cultural pulse of the community, and to see how much attention its people would give to an Indian art show. When the results were to be analyzed, it evolved that, not only had the response been unbelievably strong, but the *show itself had opened new vistas.* So-called traditional art had been included in the exhibition, but Bahah-Zhonie's painting of a kiva dance, a thorough departure from present-day Indian painting style anywhere, had found the unanimous approval of all judges as a Grand Award Winner. The other paintings were acclaimed as the "most advanced Indian painting show" anywhere in the country in the past year.

Among the nontraditional exhibits were three of Carl Gorman's favorite watercolors. For his painting, *Winter at Waterless Mountain,* he was given the show's Second Award.

A week after the closing of the exhibit, Carl received a letter from Paul Huldermann, saying he was thrilled with the success of the show and hoped Carl was happy with his own personal success. Then he went on to make an unusual request. Carl's painting, *Riders in the Storm,* had been sold not once, but twice, through a clerical error. It was a nontraditional painting of three Navajos with a leaning tree in the foreground and a mountain in the background. The second buyer still wanted it, and he asked if Carl would do another painting much like the first one; subject matter and composition should be the same. Huldermann added that the price would be the same, which was seventy-five dollars, with 10 percent going to the show. Did Carl think he could do it? If so, would he send it on, to present to the prospective buyer for his approval? "Personally," the letter concluded, "I thought this was one of the most advanced and inspired paintings in the show, and I have told everybody who wanted to listen just that."

During these years, Carl followed with great satisfaction the rising career of his son Rudolph, soon to be known as R. C. Carl always encouraged his son in his ambition to be an artist. There was no jealousy, no rivalry, only a family pride and support. If someone asked Carl about it, he would reply simply that the Navajos were always close in their families—that's the way they were.

Carl had watched the painting of his son develop its own thrust and originality, taking its themes from their Navajo origins, but moving farther away even than he had from the traditional techniques. After leaving Ganado Mission High School, R. C. had spent four years in the navy, studying at the Guam Territorial College from 1951 to 1955. Then he attended Arizona State College in 1955 (now Northern Arizona University) in Flagstaff and entered Mexico City College in 1958 (later called the University of the Americas) on a Navajo Tribal scholarship. Then he returned for further studies at San Francisco State College. By the early 1960s he had had one-man shows in the Bay Area of San Francisco. His work often bordered on the abstract, but still retained a strong "Indian" feeling. "The reservation is my source of inspiration for what I paint," R. C. said, "but I never realized this until I found myself in some far-flung place like the tip of Yucatan. Perhaps when I stay on the reservation I take too much of what it has to offer for granted. While there, I paint very little. Off the reservation, it is my realization of reality."

After the precedent-shattering success of the Scottsdale National with its outstanding exhibit of nontraditional painting (for personal reasons, R. C. chose not to show there), Carl Gorman found that his own work was beginning to be accepted in new quarters. For several

Film actor David Janssen with Carl and his painting of medicine man Frank Mitchell, Los Angeles, 1959.

82

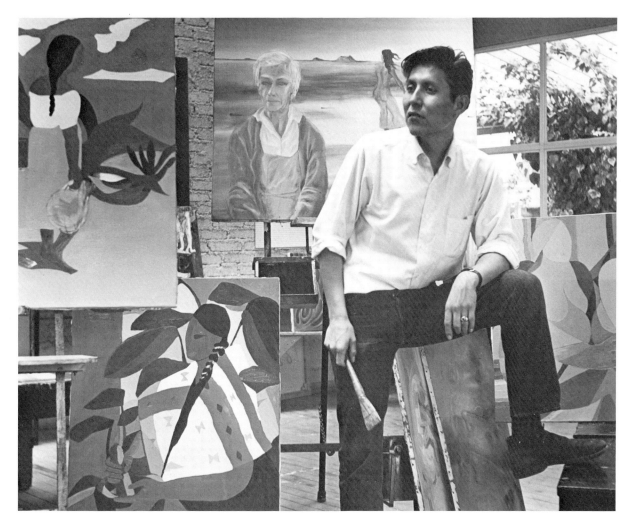

R. C. Gorman, art student, Mexico City, 1962.

years he had been encouraged by Jeanne Snodgrass, curator of American Indian art at the Philbrook Art Center in Tulsa, Oklahoma, to continue submitting entries there. She said that his work "showed great originality" and suggested that Carl and R. C. hold a father-son exhibit in the near future.

In October of 1964, the Gormans' "New Directions in American Indian Art," a father and son invitational showing, was featured at the opening of the fall museum season at the Philbrook Art Center. The exhibit included twenty-three works—ten in oil, encaustic, casein and glue, watercolor, and Venetian glass mosaic by Carl Gorman and thirteen in oil, copolymer plastic, oil-pastel, and linoleum block print by R. C. Gorman. Some of these had never been shown before; others had been prizewinners at various competitive exhibitions.

Carl and R. C. at radio interview, Tulsa, Oklahoma, 1964.

After the opening, a reception was held for the Gormans at the home of Jeanne Snodgrass, where Carl was surprised with a birthday celebration. This was the climax to a day which included his appearance on a television interview at the Tulsa State Fair, newsreel and press conferences at the Philbrook Museum, and an interview on radio. Speaking proudly, as one of the first Navajo artists to depart from the traditional Indian school of art, Carl Gorman had this to say about his work:

> The life of the Navajo is harsh and cruel, a constant
> battle with nature. Having grown up in the Navajo
> country, I am keenly aware of this and try to bring out
> some of this feeling as well as the desire to portray the
> culture of my people. I have always felt that the
> traditional school of painting is traditional to the Plains
> Indians, but not to the Navajos, and that I can better
> express my cultural heritage and myself by using
> whatever media and technique will best bring out
> whatever I want to say.

It was a triumphant time for Carl personally. He was excited by the popular reception of his work and his son's and above all with the growing critical acclaim.

In March of 1965, another "father and son" exhibit was held at the Heard Museum's Gallery of Indian Art in Phoenix, Arizona—a combined showing of forty-six works by Carl and R. C. in the varied media and materials for which they were becoming noted. "GORMANS—FATHER, SON REBELS IN INDIAN ART" was the headline caption for a feature article

84

and art critique by Joan Bucklew in the *Arizona Republic*, which praised the diversity and integrity in the work of both artists, father and son.

The people attending the show at Heard were captured by the rich, varied quality of the Gormans' work. Their subject matter was Indian, coming from their Navajo origins, the land and culture in which they took pride. But they preferred that people think of them not primarily as Indian painters. "We are painters, first and foremost," Carl Gorman said. "The subjects we have chosen are the ones we have lived."

When people asked Carl how he felt about the father-son exhibits, he said he was "happy and proud." When R. C. was asked about it, he said he had no objections to being teamed up with his famous father and added with a laugh, "None whatsoever. I need all the promotion I can get."

TEN

During these same years, the 1950s and early 1960s, when Carl Gorman's art career was maturing and commanding respect, his personal life was taking on a new direction. He became increasingly involved with the problems of the urban Navajo community in Los Angeles. A sense of obligation to his people became an ongoing concern, and with it came a growing sense of leadership and responsibility.

This was the period when Carl Gorman's philosophy was growing stronger, surer, more controlled. He was determined to succeed as an artist. He was equally determined to make it, he said, in the white man's world as a Navajo without pretending, in any sense, at any time, that he was white. He had learned that lesson of identity well at the Marine Corps training camp and in the campaigns of the South Pacific. Now, while he was living with his wife and family in the Los Angeles area, working at Douglas Aircraft, selling his paintings in the white community, forces were already at work to take him along another path, drawing him inexorably toward his own native people. The vehicle for this was the Navajo Club of Los Angeles.

During World War II, in the years from 1941 to 1945, thousands of Indians had left the reservations and gone into the big cities to take war jobs and defense work. Except for those who had gone to out-of-state boarding schools, most of them were away from their land for the first time in their lives. But they were employed and making good money. They felt pride in helping their country, in being needed, replacing men and women who had gone into military service. This represented a great change in the Navajo's relationship with the white man; for the first time they were actual participants in the white man's scene. They found themselves working side by side with people whom they had always considered outsiders, alien to their own culture and way of life.

When the war was over, this period of special employment ended abruptly. A great majority of the Navajos were forced by the lack of work to return to the reservation. They would look for jobs there, but the economic situation was a harsh one, and most would go back to the old way of life and, unfortunately, to a poverty level. Some who had acquired needed skills stayed on in their old jobs or found new ones, working out their destiny in the urban community where they had chosen to live.

During these same postwar years, hundreds of returning Indian veterans were coming into the Los Angeles area. Most had been captivated in their brief stays at training camps by the Southern California lifestyle—the little they had seen—and now they were seeking work so they could remain there permanently. Many, like Carl Gorman, were studying on the G.I. Bill at schools and colleges in Southern California. They were intent on finding a new life for themselves, away from the restricted, impoverished existence of the reservation.

The transition period was a difficult one. The spirit of idealism, of camaraderie and high endeavor that carried American society along during the war was now gone, and people were caught up once again in a materialistic way of life. When the Indian had come as a soldier in uniform, he was welcomed usually as an equal, often as a glamorous figure, extolled for his patriotism. Out of uniform, he was too often regarded with disdain, with enmity, with prejudice. The Indian was again the outsider, caught between two worlds, lonely, alienated, no longer able to feel any pride in himself.

In 1948 Carl was part of a group of Navajo men and women who attended the nondenominational American Indian Mission Church in Los Angeles. It was a good place to meet and to socialize with Indians of other tribes who lived in the area. They began to discuss among themselves the growing problems facing their people in the city. Something had to be done, they felt, not only to gain strength for themselves, but to help the many Navajos in the city adjust to Los Angeles. Where could their people go for help, companionship, advice? In addition to the handful of churches that were open to them, there was the Indian Center downtown, or the Main Street bars, where one Navajo might find another who understood the greeting "Yá' át' ééh." There he could converse in his own language, could understand and roar at a Navajo joke or talk about someone or some place back home. There was little else.

The decision was made to form the Navajo Club of Los Angeles, first proposed by Myron and Virginia Denetdale, Navajos who had come to Los Angeles before World War II. Myron had continued to work at the Lockheed Aircraft plant, and his wife, in civil service. Seeking advice on organization, they contacted the Sherman Institute in Riverside, California, the B.I.A. boarding school for Indians that they had attended. With the Denetdales on that first trip to Riverside were Elise and Jack Dover; Frank Peshlakai (Carl Gorman's uncle), son of the great silversmith and a recognized craftsman in his own right; and Ralph Roanhorse, an accomplished artist known for his watercolors. They were given sample by-laws, much encouragement, and an urgent request to help the young graduates of the Sherman Institute who were already finding difficulties of their own in making an adjustment to urban life.

The plans for the Navajo Club, from the first, were not narrow, or confined to social problems only. In a statement entitled "Objects and Policies," they wrote:

> We are to help and encourage one another and solve our
> problems; to exchange and unite our ideas and plans,
> and to share fun in our social activities; to devote
> ourselves to the study and preservation of Navajo
> history and culture; planning ways in which we may
> practicably help Navajos make social adjustment to off-
> Reservation life; keeping informed on all Tribal
> affairs. . . .

On the Navajo reservation, the economic situation was disastrous, and the population was multiplying rapidly. Reports of the extremely harsh winters of 1947–48 and 1948–49 dramatized for the American public at large the plight of the Navajo people in Arizona and New Mexico. Public opinion was aroused by articles in newspapers, national magazines, special radio programs. As firsthand news kept coming back to Los Angeles of the suffering and starvation of their people back home, the newly formed Navajo Club launched a campaign to help. It organized large shipments of food and clothing to be sent to the reservation.

For a long time, the Bureau of Indian Affairs had been deliberating a plan for the "rehabilitation" of the Navajos. This was, in fact, part of the movement generally known as "termination," which would bring to an end Indian life and culture on the reservations. By 1950, the bureau decided, with congressional approval and appropriations, to launch a full-scale relocation program for Indians who "wished to seek permanent employment opportunities away from the Reservations." Field Relocation Offices were opened in Chicago, Denver, Salt Lake City, and Los Angeles. Included in the appropriations were funds to "underwrite the costs of transportation, shipping household effects, subsistence en route to relocation destination, and subsistence for relocatees during the first few weeks at the point of relocation."

The movement of Indians from several reservations into urban communities began in February 1952. It would continue for the next seven years, and upwards of 28,000 Indians, including over 12,000 families would be "relocated." New offices would be opened in Oakland, San Francisco, St. Louis, Cleveland, and Dallas. From the beginning, there were great difficulties. In the early years of relocation, the problems that beset the Navajos in Los Angeles (as the members of the Navajo Club witnessed and recorded them) swiftly grew to overwhelming proportions. The government project began to founder badly. Navajo families were coming into Los Angeles at the rate of twenty a week, over a thousand a year. More than 6,000 people would eventually be relocated in the Los Angeles area.

The entire program was voluntary. In order to stimulate the people's decision to take part, the Bureau of Indian Affairs set up a promotion campaign with advertising and propaganda techniques. Representatives of the bureau came to the windswept Navajo reservation lands of Arizona and New Mexico with inducements for the Navajo people to leave their hogans and huts, where many were living close to starvation, and come to a rich, shining existence in a new environment. Later, in the city, the relocatees would remember, sadly, the lavish promises the government people made to them; these promises of new housing, of beautiful automobiles and bright appliances vanished in the grim urban life.

The B.I.A. men made their prepared "pitch" to large gatherings in the area chapter houses on the reservation. They set up colorful displays to bring home their points visually. They elaborated on the good jobs that were available, the high pay. They described the housing the Navajos could expect, every dwelling equipped with a large, gleaming refrigerator, a most precious possession for Navajos, who had always faced the problem of preserving food, with hot weather as a perpetual enemy. In effect, the people were told that they would have all this if they moved to Los Angeles. The men and women in the chapter houses were swayed by the extravagant promises. They signed up, by the thousands, to leave their homes and the grim problems of survival on the reservation. They went to the city—all expenses paid—as participants in the new relocation program.

In theory, on paper, the intention of the B.I.A. was to give full assistance to the "relocatees" in adjusting to the urban situation. Plans were laid out for "orientation counseling, employment procedures, family budgeting, adult education opportunities, suitable housing close to work." The whole procedure was to be directed toward "assisting the relocatees to adjust to their new environment and become self-supporting members of the community."

In fact, once the Navajo families reported to their B.I.A. office in Los Angeles, the unforeseen difficulties began. There had been no screening, no selection of applicants for relocation, and virtually all who had applied had been accepted. The great majority of the "relocatees" were uneducated by white man's standards and unskilled. A great many of them spoke no English, yet no program had been set up to teach them the language so essential for their survival in this alien urban environment. The housing that was found for the Navajo families was a far cry from the beautiful pictures portrayed. Most of the people were placed in the poorest neighborhoods in tiny apartments, crowded in with other families, or in old, run-down hotels, in single rooms. The work that was found for the men was usually many miles from their living quarters. In the huge, expanding metropolis of Los Angeles, with its inadequate transportation facilities, the Navajos met with constant problems in trying to get to and from their jobs.

The frustrations of city life for the transplanted Navajos became severe and disturbing. There was a sense of utter dislocation. They felt themselves abandoned by the B.I.A. For so many thousands who had poured into Los Angeles with high hopes, the result of the program of relocation was a social and economic disaster. With families living in slum conditions, a great number of teenage children were turning to alcohol, getting into trouble with the law. It was all too much for the people to handle. They were homesick for the land they had left, the land in which they had been born, surrounded by the Four Sacred Mountains, the land given to them by the Holy People. During the 1950s, the majority of the Navajos who came to Los Angeles drifted back to the reservation.

Almost from the beginning of the relocation, with the great influx of Navajo families, the Navajo Club became concerned with their welfare. The group had kept growing, attracting the adjusted, the well-employed, the dedicated Navajos who were resolved to help their "brothers." By the mid 1950s, they met regularly, usually once a week, in members' homes or at the YMCA in the Los Angeles suburb of Inglewood. Carl Gorman had become a leader in the club's activities. Among others in the group were Peter MacDonald, Frankie Paul, Allen Hill, Perry Allen, Tommy Anderson, and their wives. All of them were destined to go back to the Navajo reservation in the not-too-distant future, enriched and strengthened by the skills they had developed to survive in the Anglo society, and to use their expertise in leading the growing Navajo nation.

The word spread among the troubled relocatees that the Navajo Club was there as a source of help. The members were deluged with pleas from people who badly needed money or the bare necessities, or from those who needed counseling or assistance in coping with the bewildering new problems of living in the city. Navajos too proud to accept aid from outsiders or to seek public welfare would accept food, clothing, money, or guidance from another Navajo. They would even agree to seek public assistance in dire cases, but only if a reassuring "brother" or "sister" was along. Someone had to help explain things when questions fired in English were bewildering, or to clarify to a welfare interrogator why there was no birth certificate, or how one's father had only a single name instead of first and last names.

Outstanding in their efforts to improve conditions for the newcomers were the Denetdales. They went back to the offices of the B.I.A. again and again, in their desire to get the Navajo relocatees out of the slums, out of single rooms, and into apartments where they could survive as a family unit. When apartments were finally being distributed, they pointed out how vital it was to teach the people how to live in these apartments. "Navajo families," they said, "had dwelled in hogans all their lives, with no plumbing, no running water, no gas, no electricity. Now with no instruction, they were asked to live in rooms that had gas stoves and wall fireplaces; and they did not even know how to put on the gas, let alone be aware of the dangers of explosion, of fire, or carbon monoxide poisoning."

How much could a relatively small group like the Navajo Club do in such an overwhelming situation? How many people could they possibly help in the course of any given year—a few dozen, a few score, a few hundred perhaps, out of the thousands? How much money or emotional support could they provide? The club members all worked during the week and had only so much time away from their homes or families during the weekends. They tried their best to sustain the spirit of the people. They fixed up boxes of groceries, collected clothes for needy families, invited them to Thanksgiving and Christmas dinners. But more and more destitute, alienated Navajos kept besieging them. There was a limit to what the club members could do.

Even into the 1960s, the problems of the relocatees were still serious, disturbing. The officers of the Navajo Club resolved to address the administration of the tribe with a set of resolutions, presenting the conditions that continued to exist: the increase in alcoholism, crime, and juvenile delinquency; the lack of proper homes, jobs, education, or recreational facilities; the emotional difficulties, the constant frustration, and alienation. With the resolution, they urged the Navajo Tribe to join with them and the city of Los Angeles in setting up a Navajo Center (or chapter house) "to be staffed with a director, well versed in human and social and economic problems, particularly for the Navajos; a social worker, preferably with a college degree and one who can speak Navajo fluently; and the necessary office help, able to speak English and Navajo fluently." For the interim period, they asked the Navajo Tribe to appropriate a minimum of $28,000 for the 1961–62 fiscal years, "for implementing the necessary program and services so urgently needed."

The distinguished Navajo councilwoman, Annie Wauneka, who was nationally recognized and who had done so much to better social and

Navajo Club members, Los Angeles, ca. 1958. Photo by Seymour Windman.

medical conditions for her people on the reservation, was invited to come out and discuss the situation with the Navajo Club members. She came, concerned. She was willing to push it in the Tribal Council. But the problem, she indicated, with a knowledge of tribal financing, was a complicated one. The Navajo Club members needed a building first. When they got that, the tribe would fund them and give them the personnel they wanted. Unfortunately, the Navajo Club could not acquire a building without money, and ironically, they would not get any money without a building.

Carl Gorman had been active in the Navajo Club's activities for several years when he and Mary were married in March 1956. From that date on, Mary came to all the meetings. Soon she was taking part in all the discussions. She was accepted without question by all the members of the group. There was no concern about her being Anglo. As a matter of record, they all affirmed, as Carl did, that "Mary thought and acted like a good Navajo." When Carl was elected chairman of the club the following year, Mary was chosen to be secretary.

Mary was a devoted worker for the Navajo cause, ardent and articulate against the injustice that brought so many of "her people" to a state of degradation, illness, desperation. She never lost sight of the individual human beings in their plight, their need for help. She had waited a long time to marry Carl Gorman, to share his life in all its aspects. She was ready to fight for what he and she believed in together.

Long before this time, while living with her father and mother in Barstow, California, working there in the office of the Marine Corps Supply Depot, she had become concerned with the welfare of the Navajo people. She was troubled that the country at large knew so little, neither understanding nor even caring about the native American Indians. When the harsh winter months of 1947–48 brought hunger and privation to the Navajos on the reservation and awoke the sympathy of the nation, Mary felt compelled to participate, writing letters, informing people on how to help. A long letter to one of several newspapers in her home state of Rhode Island gives insight into Mary's attitude and her sensitivity toward the whole Indian problem.

Dated January 10, 1948, addressed to the editor of the *Providence Sunday Journal* in Rhode Island, it began by thanking a reader of the paper, one Mr. Diraimo of Providence, for his interest, "in the plight of our own Indians," as he had expressed it. "And that is just what the Indians would like to be," Mary wrote, "to have the feelings of being a part of this great country for which their sons fought and died so heroically during the war. . . . Surely, we should do something for these people. A collection of food and clothing for the Navajo and Hopi, as Mr. Diraimo suggests, is one way. But they need more than relief to carry them through this winter. They need a program of education, health, land improvement, and full citizenship rights, faithfully carried out, or another winter will be no different." Through treaty with the Navajos, the government had promised them these things eighty years before, Mary continued. "But promises were not kept, and the returning veterans want to know why. I believe if we honestly desire to take our place as an example and a guide to other nations on the road to world peace, we had first better settle a few old scores at home."

Now, in Los Angeles, it hurt Mary to witness the frustration and bitterness that came from the lips of the transplanted Navajos. Worst of all, she felt, were the humiliations, the lack of respect and ill-treatment they received because they were Indians. Too many Anglos still considered them unsuitable for a decent job because they were Indians.

Too many churches, whose missionaries were active on the reservation, made little effort to welcome the Indians in the city.

Of the thousands of Navajos who had come into Los Angeles in the relocation program, a small percentage stayed on with good jobs and homes. They did well materially. But they still had to solve the central problem of living in an alien society. For the members of the Navajo Club, as they tried to help and advise others, something intrinsically valuable began to happen. In the process of aiding their fellow Navajos and blood brothers, they began to be aware of a new strength in themselves as Navajos. Having lived and worked for years among the "Bila-gáana," the white people, they began to realize that their own culture was not only important to them, it was essential to their survival as whole, integrated human beings.

Here was something priceless that they had set aside or taken too much for granted back on the reservation, something the government schools and churches had taught them to look down upon because it was "Indian." They did not have to feel ashamed of a heritage like theirs because it was Indian, when it had so much strength and beauty. Already, many Anglos were beginning to ask questions of them with sincere interest, with a growing curiosity about their religion and history, about the differences between Navajos and other Indians, about their art, dress, foods, dances. Invitations came to them to exhibit Navajo arts and crafts at various shows, local fairs, and gallery showings, to demonstrate Navajo sandpainting, weaving, silversmithing.

Carl Gorman's Indian paintings, jewelry, and mosaics, on display at the gem and mineral shows in Los Angeles attracted the attention and admiration of Anglo crowds. His exhibits, sponsored by the Navajo Club, won first place awards at two art shows: in May 1960, with watercolors of horses at the Great Western Livestock show in Los Angeles; in June with his oils and ceramic pieces at the Los Angeles Hobby show.

The white community was exposed to a truer picture of the Indian of today, in contrast to the stereotyped Hollywood version. The Navajo Club was asked by several groups and churches if they would present authentic Navajo dances, in native costume. The members accepted the challenge. It meant a whole new area of research and training. Carl Gorman was appointed the leader of the project. He found several old songs that went with the Navajo dances. The club members, especially the Denetdales, searched back into their memories and came up with others. They learned and rehearsed the songs and then taped them. Trips to the reservation brought back more. Carl had the idea of training a team of young Navajo girl dancers. They were dressed in the colorful old style, the Navajo woven dress known as the "beal." Carl didn't feel it would be proper to have a traditional Navajo Yei-bi-chei song for a contemporary dance. Wanting that rhythm, he selected instead an old version of the Yei-bi-chei made up by the Hopis around 1917. With six girls and a young Navajo singer, Douglas Mitchell, he choreographed a new dance and called it the "Gourd Rattle Dance."

With both the traditional dances and the young people's modern versions, the Navajo Club met an enthusiastic reception wherever they went. They put on numerous performances in Los Angeles. They were asked to do a television show. The tribute, they felt, was not only to their showmanship or their well-rehearsed performance. It was an acceptance of them as Navajos and of their authentic culture.

The commissioner of the Navajo Tribal Fair, Howard Gorman (no relation of Carl Gorman), invited the Navajo Club dance team in 1962 to participate in the night performance at the annual fair at Window Rock, Arizona, the capital of the Navajo nation. The decision was made to go back to the reservation with their dances and songs. In some cases, the Navajo Club had to intervene and officially ask employers for time off so the dancers could perform at Window Rock. For some it meant a loss of pay. But the opportunity to appear at the annual Navajo fair was something none of the performers wanted to miss. Every Navajo throughout the reservation who could possibly come by truck or wagon, by horseback or on foot, would be there.

As Mary reported to the full membership on returning to Los Angeles, the Navajo Club ensemble took the fair by storm. They won all the prizes for dances. They received ovations as they came back again and again for encores. The elderly people in the crowds at the fairgrounds, watching the old dances done once again, were enchanted with the sight of it all, with the old songs and the traditional costumes of the men and women. They were touched with memories out of their own past. A woman came over to Carl Gorman, who had been in all the dances, pouring his inexhaustible energy into them. She was crying as she spoke to him. She was the mother of four of the girls in the team. She kept saying, over and over again in Navajo, "We won! We won!" A medicine man, an old friend of Carl's, told him years later that he had brought his own team of dancers to Window Rock every year and that they had always taken first prize. But he had decided at the time not to bring them anymore because "that crazy bunch from Los Angeles was too good!"

It was a return to the old times, Mary Gorman said to the club, a triumph for their people. This was the beginning of a revival of interest in their history and their heritage. It had come at the right time for everyone, especially for themselves. Here they were, a group of people who were employed, educated, many of them talented, with a serious desire to make a place for themselves in the Anglo world. In the years after World War II they were determined to merge with the whites totally,

Carl, Los Angeles, 1959. For many years he signed his paintings Kin-ya-onny-beyeh (son of Towering House People).

and the more successful they became, the more they tried to think white, to become assimilated, as their government wanted them to. But the process had failed them. They had found their own lives complicated, often troubled. Now the members of the Navajo Club were confronting this squarely, and their efforts at establishing their own identity within an urban setting were bearing fruit. They had won the respect and praise of the Anglo community. They could truly think of themselves unashamedly as Navajos, wherever they worked, wherever they might go.

And they were responsible for something else. With the outstanding success of their dances, songs, and costumes on the reservation, a renewed interest in Navajo heritage slowly began to emerge in the population there. Like the Navajos in the urban centers, too many here had ignored their own Indian identity. They had returned from government schools or from wartime service with feelings of inferiority, of distrust, of hurt at not being accepted completely in the white man's world. At the coming of the Navajo Club performers, with their vibrant revival of "the old things," people on the reservation began to realize that they had something of their own, "truly Navajo" to hold onto. Groups became interested in the old songs; they started copying the old-style (beal) costumes the young girls had worn in the Navajo dances, and people

97

could be seen wearing them. They encouraged their children to speak Navajo; they renewed interest in their own arts and crafts. They felt the richness and color of their people's background returning into their daily lives.

A new attitude was emerging, a new direction for Navajos who had been taking a personal satisfaction in how "white" they could think, how "modern" they could be. Young Navajo men and women, graduates of colleges and schools of professional training, were returning to work on the reservation in larger numbers, speaking of "service to their people," filled perhaps for the first time in their lives with a sense of belonging, of pride in being Navajo.

Members of the Navajo Club began to go back to the reservation, one by one, to remain there permanently. They were drawn by the coming of a new reform administration, headed by Raymond Nakai, the outspoken candidate for chairman. Perry Allen left his legal work in Los Angeles to work as chief campaign coordinator. When Nakai was elected, he created an Office of Methods Management and Procedures. Peter MacDonald left Hughes Aircraft, where he was an engineer, to take charge of that office, the first step in his move upwards in the Navajo political scene. Others were to follow, young Navajos like Allen Hill, Tommy Anderson, Frankie Paul, men with education and training who would move up into positions of importance in their native land.

As early as 1960, Carl Gorman considered coming back to the Navajo reservation to set up a studio to work and to teach. In an interview with the Gallup, New Mexico *Independent*, on the occasion of his art show in that city, he said,

> I want to help my Navajo people preserve their beautiful arts and crafts, which are rapidly vanishing. Indian art is dying out and we Navajo people must do something to prevent this great loss. Our young Navajo people do not realize the valuable heritage they have. They need training and help. Art offers them an opportunity to do creative work; and at the same time their earnings can be enough to support them if they have the initiative and the industry.

His intent was serious. The dream remained constant. But he did not rush the change in his way of life. Time eventually indicated the role he was to play in the lives of his people.

ELEVEN

Almost from the moment Alfred Kee Gorman was born in 1957, Carl and Mary exposed him to their art world. They took little Kee to his first art show when he was three months old. As soon as he could hold a crayon in his small fist, he was drawing. When he was less than three years old, he did his first easel painting. He worked beside his father in the studio, in the garage of their home, holding a paintbrush in his hand, listening with Carl to the records of opera music that played continually. "He loved to paint," Mary said to friends, "the way other children love to play ball."

They were now living in their home in Northridge, California at the upper end of the San Fernando Valley, a section far from the congestion of the city, but still part of the extended Los Angeles community. An open field lay across the street. A grocery store was on the corner, a school a block away. Kee could walk to kindergarten from his home. The people about them were congenial and pleasant. One neighbor had an auto repair shop in his garage, where Carl would take his car to be fixed. Another was a theatrical agent whose music groups came often to his home, and Carl would drop in when they were performing. Kee went over to the agent's house every day to sit on his horse.

The Gorman home was crowded with people, with joy, with problems. Mary's mother, emotionally disturbed since the death of her husband, was living with them. So were two Navajo girls who were placed by the county in a Navajo home following hospitalization. One stayed for a number of months until she married and went back to the reservation; the other one made her home in the Los Angeles area. Meetings

Zonnie, Northridge, California, 1964.

of the Navajo Club were held in their home on many occasions, as well as committee or executive board meetings, or special meetings with a woman lawyer from Los Angeles who volunteered to take Navajo cases.

On weekends, when Carl wasn't painting, the Gorman family visited with friends, or frequently went to see Uncle Frank Peshlakai at his silversmith shop on Olvera Street in Los Angeles. They went to art exhibits, to the beach, to the Indian center, or to Japanese restaurants where Carl loved to eat. Sometimes they went to the desert and to Barstow to see his brother Steve.

At the age of four, Kee "showed" with his father in a local exhibition in Northridge. A painting of his sold. When he was five, he did a mosaic and sold that. Someone asked him if he was going to be an artist when he grew up, and Kee answered simply, "I am an artist." At six years of age in 1963, he won the Margretta S. Dietrich Memorial Award for contemporary Indian Artist in his age group, with a painting in tempera called *Wild Deer*. One of the jurors, Richard Pritzloff, purchased the painting himself, and he presented it to the Fine Arts Museum of New Mexico. Kee's fingerpainting of flowers took a first place award for ages six to twelve in the 1963 Navajo tribal fair in Window Rock.

That same year on May 15, Zonnie was born, a beautiful dark-eyed child. From the beginning, secure in her cradleboard, she went everywhere with the family. In late summer, the Gormans traveled to the

Navajo reservation for the showing of Carl's work and Kee's at the Window Rock fair. When it was over, they set out northward in their station wagon toward Chinle and Canyon de Chelly. The September morning sky was a dazzling blue. They passed through the forest of Ganado Ridge, at an elevation of almost eight thousand feet, where mile upon mile of dark green spruce and fir and ponderosa pine was dotted with fields of yellow rabbit bush. Beyond this was the endless gray-green sage. Then they were on the high plateau, the narrow two-way highway stretching ribbon-straight into the limitless distance, the land falling away on the right to the soft, undulating patches of multicolored desert, called the "Beautiful Valley" by their people. On the left, the low buff ground rose imperceptibly toward the distant, looming mass of Black Mesa. Overhead, and all around, before and behind them, was the great blue covering of the sky—and as always for Carl, a sense of rediscovering the beauty and magnificence of it. He felt again the truth and the meaning of this personal sky, this all-enveloping canopy that surrounded and protected his Navajo world.

Carl touched Kee on the shoulder, then pointed to the landscape ahead. A few years ago, he said, he had given a lift to a man on this same road, an Anglo businessman who asked Carl if he could be dropped off at Fleming Begay's trading post in Chinle. The man kept staring out of the window of the car. Absolutely nothing out there, he said, nothing but a wasteland. How could the Navajos stand it? What did his father say? Kee asked. Did he try to tell the man anything? Carl shook his head. "What could I say to him? Do you think if that man came back here a thousand times, Kee," he said, "do you think he would ever see anything but a wasteland? How could I talk to him about the beauty of this land—yours and mine?"

Kee had grown up in the city. Carl wanted him to begin to know the land, to experience the overwhelming sense of space, to feel his belonging in a world full of light and color, alive and shimmering with a vitality all its own. One day, Carl thought, Kee too would come to know and love, as he did, the immense variety of Navajo landscape, the buttes and soaring monuments and deep canyons and azure lakes and distant mountains. He would come to know the fullness of the land as well as its people, and understand that the two were one, that there was no separation, but a wholeness in beauty that pervaded and encompassed all things. Who could tell, too, how much the sensitivity to all this might affect, might pervade Kee's painting, as it had done R. C.'s, as it had done his own, for so many years now?

When they came to Chinle, they turned off toward the big stone house his father had built back in 1918. Mary and Zonnie, who was still in a cradleboard, stayed here while Carl and Kee went off. Carl had looked forward to this day, the two of them together.

Left, Kee at his easel, Northridge, 1960; *right,* Kee, Northridge, 1961.

They drove along a dusty road until they came to a small, square adobe trading post. That was the way it looked, Carl said to Kee, his own father's main trading post. But it had been torn down a long time before. They went up a narrow dirt road, to a high patch of ground overlooking the broad wash that led from Canyon de Chelly. They got out of the station wagon. Carl pointed to a clearing, surrounded by tall cottonwood trees. That was the spot, he said, the place where the post stood. Was that where he grew up? Kee asked. "That was the place," Carl said. "But I wasn't born there." He turned Kee around, to face eastward, toward an endless vista of hills and dust. About eight miles that way, on the road to Nazlini, Carl said, his father had set up his second trading post and that's where he was born. He was going back to the place of his own beginning, taking Kee back with him. He spoke of his mother coming out there, alone with his father on the long trek from Fort Defiance, to build the trading post and raise a family. "My mother must have had a lot of strength," he said. "I guess she got it from her own father. He was a great leader, you know, a great silversmith." He began to speak of his grandfather Peshlakai to Kee, just as his father before had spoken to him of the old leader's artistry, his skill and eminence. Here again was the telling of one's heritage, proudly, from one generation to the next.

Later, as they passed through the wonders of Canyon de Chelly, Carl was to tell his son the same stories he had heard from his own parents: of the treacherous quicksands in the canyon, of the Spanish soldiers coming to massacre the people living there, of the heroic tales and

102

Kee, Northridge, 1963.

tragedy of Fortress Rock. Inevitably, he spoke of the terror and hardships
of the Long Walk and the ensuing imprisonment at Fort Sumner. The
boy Kee listened entranced, as Carl himself had once been, always asking
to hear more.

They came to the Antelope Ruins, and Carl told of the ancient people
who had lived there. Kee was enchanted at the sight of the pictographs
on the high canyon walls, the antelopes leaping one by one forever away
from him. Far up Canyon del Muerto, they stopped before Standing Cow
Ruin. Kee's eyes fastened on the huge, painted black-and-white cow on
the wall that gave the place its name. He stood for a long time before

103

the painting nearby of the Spanish cavalry unit, the horses and soldiers in armor, and the robed priest accompanying them. He wondered who had done it, and Carl told him about the painter who was a small boy like Kee when he saw the Spaniards coming through the canyon and how, forty years later, he painted those same Spaniards on the canyon wall, for his people to remember the story of the massacre.

All the way on the drive home to California, Kee was restless. From time to time, he made quick sketches on his drawing pad. When the Gormans arrived back in Northridge, Kee painted in acrylic his impressions of what he had seen on the canyon rocks that day. He called it *Visit to Canyon de Chelly Gallery.*

The painting was exhibited the following year at the Scottsdale Indian Art exhibit in 1964. It won a first prize in the juvenile division and was also selected to receive the Elkus Memorial Award for incentive. Kee continued to enter exhibitions with his father, winning awards. One or more of his paintings were sold each time he showed.

Kee's half-brother, the artist known as R. C. by now, was captivated by the talent of the bright, enthusiastic child. When he visited with the family in Northridge, he invariably spent time in his father's studio. One evening Carl and Kee were painting, each at his own easel. R. C. picked up a brush, did a quick painting of a watermelon. Kee was watching him. When R. C. had finished, Kee said that wasn't the way to paint a watermelon. He wasn't being rude. He was quietly saying what he thought, as one artist to another. R. C. laughed at the criticism. All right, he said, why didn't Kee go ahead and show him how? In ten minutes, Kee painted a watermelon, and R. C. looked at it critically. "It's good," he said. "It's better than mine." He asked Kee if he could have it to keep, and Kee gave it to him.

"That boy is great," he said to Carl the next day, as he was leaving to go back to his studio in San Francisco. "I think he'll be a superb artist. You'll see, Dad, he'll be better than all of us."

TWELVE

The schedule of activity Carl Gorman had taken upon himself in the early 1960s was as extensive as he was enthusiastic in pursuing it. The more energy he expended, the more he seemed to thrive. He was still working in his regular job as a technical artist at Douglas Aircraft in Santa Monica. He was painting nights and weekends, as well as exhibiting and traveling to further his art career. He and Mary never let up in their Navajo Club work, helping relocatees, trying to provide Navajo lecturers, weavers, craftsmen in an "enlightened program" for the Anglo community. In California, New Mexico, and Arizona, both on the reservation and off, Carl Gorman found himself steadily in the public forum. He continued to speak out forcefully on behalf of his people and to them. His ideas on Navajo culture development, as well as his skill as an artist who was breaking new ground, drew public attention to him.

Late in 1962, Carl's work at Douglas Aircraft came to an end. It happened in a strange way.

A close friend, George Tatgenhorst, who was working as a technical illustrator at the RocketDyne plant in the San Fernando Valley, suggested to Carl that he try to come to work there. Carl thought it a great idea. He would be close to his home in Northridge instead of making the long drive across town each day to the Douglas plant in Torrance, to which he had been transferred.

He applied for a job at RocketDyne, and he was accepted. But since he was working for Douglas on a government contract, there would be a waiting period of three months, he was told, before he could be hired. Carl quit Douglas, worked on his art for the three months, then went

Fabric design by Carl at Otis, Los Angeles, 1954.

back to RocketDyne, only to find their contract had run out and no jobs were available.

However, Carl actually welcomed the opportunity to be free, to put all his time into his art. There was much he wanted to paint now, so many new areas he wanted to explore. The year 1963 was the most productive time of his entire career. He did many of the works that were later to be exhibited, including the breakthrough paintings shown at Philbrook and Heard. For a time he put all his concentration into mosaics, making tables and plaques, with Mary and Kee helping him in the studio. This was a year, too, when Carl was able to spend a great deal of time painting with Kee.

Like so many artists, Carl had the dream of building a successful commercial enterprise that would draw on his talents and give him financial freedom to pursue new creative areas. In partnership with Mel (who was half Navajo) and Connie Gardner, whom they had met at tribal fairs, Carl and Mary set up a silk-screening business which would make extensive use of Indian symbols in designing fabrics. The partnership lasted for a year. They had several contracts with the Navajo Tribe when they decided mutually to dissolve the business because they felt there would be a conflict of interest. Mel Gardner had gone to work for the tribe, and Carl was appointed to an important position on the Navajo reservation, one that he wanted very much, one that would give him the opportunity to be of direct influence in the lives of his own people.

106

Crucifixion. 1950s. Oil on plyboard. 40×35 inches.

Peshlakai, Chicago World's Fair, 1893.

Nelson Gorman. 1958. Oil on canvas. 22 × 28 inches.

Navajo Squaw Dance. Mosaic tile. 29 × 41 inches. Cover of *Westways*
Magazine, August 1962. Courtesy of the Automobile Club of Southern
California.

Not Allowed. 1950s. Oil on canvas. 45 × 35 inches.

Riders of the Storm. 1962. Watercolor. 30×22 inches. Courtesy of the Heard
Museum, Phoenix, Arizona.

Cutting Horses Out. 1970. Watercolor. 30 × 24 inches.

Black Pot Drum of Evening Way. 1971. Oil on canvas. 60×84 inches.
Courtesy of the Heard Museum, Phoenix, Arizona.

114

Carl, Northridge, 1963, before his appointment as director
of the Navajo Arts and Crafts Guild.

On February 11, 1964, Carl Gorman was selected by the Resources
Office of the Navajo Tribe to become the new director of the Navajo
Arts and Crafts Guild. He was returning to the reservation as head of a
tribal enterprise that was dedicated to the same ideals he believed in:
"to bring a deeper respect for their native art to the Navajo people and
a renewed faith in their ability to earn their living in it."

This was a time of high expectations for Carl and Mary Gorman,
of satisfaction in their work, of pleasure in their family closeness, with
Kee who was seven, and Zonnie who was nine months old. They were
coming back to live on the reservation, to Window Rock, the capital of
the Navajo nation. They were provided a tribal duplex, and they eventually bought a trailer for a studio and put it behind the house. They

had no furniture at first, only camping gear, and Zonnie slept in her playpen. It was three months before they were able to go to California and bring back their furniture.

Carl started his work as director in the new beautifully designed building that housed the Navajo Arts and Crafts Guild. He came in on a wave of congratulations. Interest in minority groups was burgeoning throughout the country. At long last Indians were being looked upon by many people as citizens of this country who deserved to be treated with dignity and respect. Tributes poured in to Carl Gorman, not only from the Navajo reservation and from his "brothers" in the Los Angeles area; they came from high political dignitaries, from Senator Barry Goldwater of Arizona, and from senators Tom Kuchel and Clair Engel of California. A personal letter to Carl from Stewart J. Udall, secretary of the interior, wished him success and offered the cooperation of his department to the Navajo Arts and Crafts Guild.

As far back as 1940, the Navajos had been concerned about maintaining high standards for their craftsmen, and finding a way to procure better financial rewards for their work. In that year, the Arts and Crafts Guild was founded. Its first manager was the scholar and anthropologist John Adair, long recognized for his appreciation and knowledge of Indian arts. His assistant was Ambrose Roanhorse, an exceptionally skilled Navajo craftsman. The two made an excellent start at organization. World War II disrupted their work, but in the years after the war, the guild was reestablished. In 1951, it became an official Navajo enterprise. The brilliant, young Ned Hatathli, who had trained under Anglo managers, was selected to be the first Navajo director. Responding to his management, more and more weavers and silvermakers brought their rugs and jewelry into the old log building on the fairgrounds to be put up for sale. Eventually, the plain structure was replaced by a splendid new one, built by the tribe in Window Rock. Ned Hatathli was to become a member of the Tribal Council, then director of Tribal Resources, and finally in the late 1960s, first president of the new Navajo Community College.

When Carl Gorman became manager of the guild in 1964, he followed an Anglo director, Russ Lindgren. As a Navajo, Carl was determined to further the ideals set forth by Ned Hatathli, to discontinue large purchases from the traders, and to buy more work directly from the Navajo artists and craftsmen. He met with the men and women in their homes, in their places of work, in their chapter houses. He spoke to them in Navajo, conveying his feelings for color, design, and a sense of the beautiful. He encouraged his people to aim for the highest quality, much as his grandfather Peshlakai had done two generations before him.

The best silversmiths and rug weavers began to come to the guild at Window Rock from different regions of the reservation. The word went out that the prices were honest and fair. Also, they would be paid in cash, no waiting, no delays. Carl Gorman assured his artists that the guild would protect their interests, display their work, and bring them the money they really deserved. This had been a prime reason in having a guild from them in the first place, he said; it was part of the original philosophy. He was sorry it hadn't always been put into practice. Here at the guild, he asserted, the artists would get the major share of what came in for their work. "It's the way you deserve," he said, and the word would spread, on how beautiful their Navajo rugs and silver jewelry were. Tourists would come in greater numbers from all over to buy them. The day would come, he prophesied, when Navajo art works would be displayed and sold, not just in a few places, but in stores throughout America. He knew his people and the worth of their products. The time for what he predicted came even sooner than he thought— in the next few years.

He spent countless hours encouraging young Navajo people of talent. In May 1964, the guild opened its annual student exhibit, an event started in 1961 by Martin Link, director of the Navajo Museum, and taken over the next year by the guild. Young artists sent in their work representing thirteen schools in Arizona, New Mexico, Utah, Oklahoma, and California. In June, the guild announced the dedication and opening of a new sales and display shop at Cameron, Arizona, to be managed by Kenneth Begay, a noted Navajo silversmith, and his wife Eleanor. The Begays carried out Carl Gorman's policies, reaching out to contact and personally encourage the weavers and silversmiths in their area.

Carl worked indefatigably to promote and publicize the guild products, its wholesale and mail order business as well as its retail sales. Unlike his predecessors, he traveled extensively to do so. At the invitation of the Prescott, Arizona Centennial Commission, he sponsored an exhibit of Navajo weavers and silversmiths, displaying their works daily, in the city plaza. He answered questions about the people's work, gave interviews, and took orders. He had as his assistants two Navajo students who were with the guild under the tribal summer employment program. The following year he went to Bristol, Rhode Island with Mary and their two children visiting her family. It was his first trip to the east coast, and in an interview on Indian arts to the local newspaper, the *Phoenix*, the reporter noted that the Gormans were in New England in conjunction with the American Indian Festival held in Boston, where the Navajo Arts and Crafts Guild of which Mr. Gorman was manager, would be exhibiting.

In this same time period, the two father-son exhibits Carl had held with R. C.—at the prestigious Philbrook Art Center in Tulsa, Oklahoma and at the Heard Museum in Phoenix—had been unqualified successes. R. C. was already becoming recognized as having extraordinary talent and was headed for a strong career of his own. As for young Kee, he was showing continually, winning more awards, selling his work. Painting alongside Carl, he absorbed knowledge and instructions from his father like a confirmed protégé. But Carl respected Kee's inner spirit and his feelings for art; he let the boy follow his own inclinations in what he chose to do.

Late in 1965, Kee received a personal letter from the reputable Manchester Gallery in Taos, New Mexico. Hand-written by the owner, it read:

> Kee Gorman, Esquire
> Window Rock, Arizona
>
> Dear Kee:
>
> Yesterday I sold two of your paintings: *Watermelons* and *The Dragon.* They came to $65.00. The Gallery has taken out ¹/₃ commission of $21.67 and encloses a check for you of the balance of $43.33.
>
> When are you going to paint some more for us?
>
> Please tell your Mother that I talked to Mrs. Massey in Washington on the telephone a couple of days ago. Your Father's painting arrived safely and on time. They were excited about it in Washington.
>
> Let me hear if you are doing some more good painting.
>
> My regards to your family.
>
> Sincerely,
>
> (signed) John Manchester

Early one July morning in 1966, the Gorman family set out for Albuquerque in a newly purchased Volkswagon camper to have the car serviced. Mary was driving. Carl was in the front seat beside her, dozing. The two children and Mary's mother were asleep in the back. They were about one hundred miles from Window Rock. The sun was just coming up. Mary drowsed momentarily at the wheel. The car suddenly veered to the left, out of control. Carl grabbed at the wheel, trying to straighten it, but the camper spun off the pavement and turned over three times. Everybody was thrown out. A passing car stopped to help them. An emergency ambulance came and raced with Kee, Zonnie, and Mary's mother, all three unconscious, to the nearest hospital in the small town of Grants, New Mexico. Then it returned for Carl and Mary. By the time they reached the hospital, Kee was dead.

Mary's mother remained unconscious and died some days later.

Portrait of his father in hospital, by R. C. Gorman, 1966.

Grief. R. C. Gorman, 1967.

R. C. and Carl, San Francisco, 1966.

Zonnie and Mary both suffered concussions and minor injuries. Carl's condition was critical, with a badly shattered pelvis. He remained in the hospital for more than two months. After two weeks, Mary and Zonnie were able to leave the hospital. People in Grants were concerned and helpful, and found a motel room for them. R. C. came down from San Francisco and stayed with them at the motel. He visited his father every day.

When Carl heard from Mary that their son Kee had died, his first words were that he would never paint again. His depression was severe and prolonged, his spirit totally crushed. R. C. brought drawing pads and pencils for Carl, but they were ignored. He put his own feelings into a stark, poignant drawing entitled "Grief."

For weeks on end Carl was in great physical pain; his body was in traction and mended very slowly. The doctors declared privately to Mary that they were afraid he would never be able to walk normally again. Mary never told her husband. She knew something of the power within him. Despite the harshness of the tragedy, she was certain his spirit would begin to restore itself and he would fight back. He did. When he left the hospital, he walked out on crutches. Within a month, he was using only a cane. By early November, he was shoveling snow.

Carl returned to his job as director of the Navajo Arts and Crafts Guild. Dealing with artists and craftsmen again, it was hard for him to forget or ignore his own shattered emotions. Every artist reminded him of his Kee, and the loss of Kee. Only Mary's support, despite her own grief, and the presence of Zonnie sustained him. After some time had passed, Mary tried to talk to him about painting again. He would find comfort in that, she said, if he would only try. But he shook his head.

"Every time I look at a brush," he said, "if I even think of a brush, I think of Kee. I can't help it. I see him beside me. I think of what he would be painting."

R. C. came to visit his father in Window Rock. He tried again to encourage Carl to go back to his art. They could have another show together, he said. People loved Carl Gorman's paintings; they had bought practically everything he ever exhibited. "You've got to do it, Dad," he pleaded. "Let's try it again. We'll do it together." His urging had no more success than Mary's. There were no arguments or logic to persuade his father.

At this point of crisis in his life, Carl Gorman was a man without a central force. He could not draw or paint. He would not lift a brush. Without his art, he felt purposeless. He was almost sixty years old, and he was drifting again.

THIRTEEN

Carl Gorman had been back at work for a month, unable to function as he used to, when a friend came to visit him and said there was a job that he ought to apply for, that he was the right man for it. The opening was in ONEO, Overall Navajo Economic Opportunity, a program funded by the U.S. government on a three-year grant. Peter MacDonald had just been appointed as its head by Tribal Chairman Nakai.

Carl applied and was hired in November 1966. The new program had awakened his interest. It was to develop and guide a project in Navajo cultural studies: to put together for the first time, in book form, a true history of the Navajo people, created for them and to be written on a high-school level. The basic method was to gather legends and stories from the older people themselves who had in turn heard them from their forebears. Young men and women were picked by Carl to go out and make tape recordings of what "elderlies" and the medicine men would tell them. In this oral transmission, the history of the people had always been preserved, treasured in their minds and memories, and transmitted from generation to generation by way of their spoken words.

Carl formed an advisory board of eighteen medicine men (fifteen men and three women) all steeped in the history and lore of the Navajo. Some were diagnosticians, gifted, intuitive people who called upon the Holy Ones for their inspiration, but who also were skilled in gleaning information from their patients or members of the family. Several were both diagnosticians and herbalists with an extensive knowledge of plants, herbs, and drugs, handed down from centuries past. A number were the Hataathlii, or "singers," the "priests" who conducted the ceremonials, chanted religious songs, interpreted the mythical stories. They staged the entire healing "sings," which could last two, five, or nine nights—a tremendous artistic accomplishment, comparable to learning the score and production of an entire Wagnerian opera and knowing all the parts by heart. The Hataathlii was also responsible, in many ceremonials, for the intricate sandpaintings, which were in support of the patient and drawn on the floor of the hogan.

The members of the advisory board were carefully selected from the five agencies or districts into which the Navajo reservation had been early divided. Among those who became his close friends were Dene-tsosie and Curly Mustache, brothers from Wheatfields; Frank Goldtooth from Tuba City; Chahadin Benally from Many Farms; Jean Murphy, Danny and Tom Ration from Crownpoint; Opal Descheeney and David Kindle from Shiprock. Carl's advisory board met each month, sometimes at ONEO headquarters in Fort Defiance, more often in the local communities of the members. They held lengthy discussions on the historical material, weighing and evaluating the stories that came in from that field. The wives almost always came along, never hesitating to interrupt to make points of their own.

Mary went to many of the meetings with Carl. The dialogue was in Navajo, of which she understood little, but afterwards, she would enthusiastically discuss with Carl everything that had been said. This was a fascinating new form of research for her. When these people were all gathered together, exchanging lore and legends, within their minds and memories was a unique repository of knowledge. Here was a wealth of source material on the history and culture of the Navajo people, and it was as valuable, she felt, as the material found in the books and documents of our great libraries.

While Carl was involved in this new absorbing work, R. C. was still searching for a way to bring his father back into the art world. An opportunity came when a series of exhibitions of Indian art was planned for the new headquarters and gallery at the American Indian Historical Society in San Francisco. The first one arranged was a father and son exhibition for Carl and R. C. R. C. persuaded Carl to let some of his work be shown and to come to San Francisco for the opening in August 1967. With Carl, Mary, and their daughter, Zonnie, was David Kindle, the Navajo historian and diagnostician and member of Carl's advisory board.

Kindle opened the showing with a Navajo blessing ceremony. Afterwards, when R. C. took his family and his special guest to a prominent restaurant for dinner, the maitre d' said that Kindle could not be admitted because he did not have on the required necktie. R. C. pointed to the traditional turquoise necklace Kindle was wearing, "You have to

Carl, medicine man Chahadin Benally, Many Farms, Arizona, 1974.

let him in," he said. "He is as dressed in his culture as you are in yours."
Without another word, they were all led to their table.

In the ONEO project, which Carl headed, more than a thousand
tapes were ultimately recorded. The young Navajo researchers who went
into the field came back with countless stories. Many of them were
family tales, or grandparents' recollections of the bitter Fort Sumner
period when they were "imprisoned" far from their native land. The
most valuable of the tapes were those that dealt with the older legends,
the myths, the history. "If you're writing history," said one medicine
man to Carl, "you have to pull it out of the myth. The myth contains
the history of the tribe."

When it was time to put all the gathered material in book form,
the three years were up. Money for the program had run out, and no
more would be forthcoming. It was a project without a consummation.
To this day, a transcript of the tapes has been held at the Window Rock
public library, under lock and key, by ONEO order.

But for Carl and Mary it had been a personal salvation. It not only took their thoughts and feelings beyond the emptiness and grief of losing Kee, it carried them back in time into an exploration of the rich lore and legends of the Navajo past. It was eventually to lead them into a more thorough study of the religion, history, and philosophy of the Navajo, such as few of their own people had the opportunity to pursue.

The real source of their knowledge was less from the tapes that were recorded than from the meetings held with the eighteen members of the advisory board. Carl would listen to the stories told, examined, retold; he asked questions; he probed into the meaning of the material. He engaged in long dialogues with the learned medicine men, who had their own stories involving history and culture contained in the different ceremonials. He met with them in their homes, on different parts of the reservation. When they were in Fort Defiance for meetings, he often invited them to come for lunch to his trailer home, a few miles away in St. Michael's. They talked for hours, and he learned from them.

They went deep into the history of the Anasazi people who lived in their land a thousand or more years ago, in the canyons and the cliffs. But who were the "old ones" and what were they really like? Were they truly Navajo ancestors? In the books of the white man, the Navajos were described as a tribe coming down into this territory about the fifteenth or sixteenth century, just ahead of the Spaniards, who called them "Apache de Nabehu." But the historians in Carl's group of advisors pointed out that in the old legends their people had always been there. They analyzed the word *Anasazi*. In Navajo it translates to "stranger-relatives." It can also mean enemies but not in this case, they said. Those ancient people could well be the forebears of some of the Navajo clans.

Living today in the area between the Four Sacred Mountains, most of the original clans, such as the Kin-ya-onny, trace the history of their clans by root names back to the time of the Anasazi period.

The Hataathlii, the "singers" among the group, spoke of ancient "white house ruins" that were mentioned in the ceremonials. There were three known as such in the Navajo region: one in a canyon about twenty miles from Kayenta, another in Colorado near the Mancos River, and the third in Canyon de Chelly. According to the myths, the Yei-bi-chei lived under the rocks in Canyon de Chelly; so, in time, the beautiful White House Ruins in the cliffs of this canyon became known as the place where the Nine-Night Chant, the Yei-bi-chei originated. In the Navajo religious legends, said the Hataathlii, many things are recounted that happened when these old, sacred places were at their height. They are part of the Navajo heritage and give the people of today a sense of belonging, a connection with the ancient ones and their places.

The discussions often centered upon what happened to the "old ones" who inhabited ancient pueblos and cliff dwellings. Why had they left? Did anyone really know? The white man's documents, they said, described the years of terrible drought around the end of the thirteenth century and pointed to enemies of the cliff-dwelling people. But nothing seemed to explain fully enough the swift changes that took place in that ancient time. The old legends of the Navajos told of floods, terrible fires, volcanos setting off poisonous gases and ash fallout. The Navajo historians talked of a time of catastrophe, "the time when the mountains smoked." The medicine woman Opal Descheeney recalled a legend about Mesa Verde, and the "flood of gas" when people couldn't breathe. A legend from the Chaco Canyon settlements told of a volcano whose lava flow cut off the only river that ran through that ancient community of almost six thousand people. Any one of those disasters could have started a mass migration to other places.

Where *did* the people go? No one knew for certain. Some of the Navajo legends made reference to the West Coast, and trails to the Great Ocean. In one ceremonial chant, the historian David Kindle pointed out there were descriptions of landscape all the way from the Pacific to what is New Mexico today. Why should there be these descriptions— how could there be—unless they were based on fact? Perhaps the ancestors of the Navajo people left their dwellings to make the trek westward, and their descendants, at some later time, returned to the Southwest.

The Gormans were fascinated and enriched by these personal accounts of legendary history. Mary was greatly stimulated by what the old legends revealed. She began her own research, going to the public library at Gallup, studying the archeological and anthropological records of the Navajo people, their land and their origins. There was an urgent need, she saw, to set up a genuine correlation between those records with their historical data and what all the old tales revealed. It was a project she was to work on for many years to come.

Carl saw more clearly now what the medicine men meant when they said that the myths contained a great deal of the historical background of the Navajos. "They straightened me out," he said to Mary one night. "With our people, the history and the religion are one, all interwoven. That's the way it has always been."

His mind expanded with the amazing wealth of Navajo culture that was being opened up to him by the circle of learned people. He began to understand the depth and complexity of his religion that went back thousands of years, long before the birth of Christianity—the elemental stories of Creation, the concept of a Supreme Being and a world endowed with his spirit, and of the Holy People who were meant to be the intermediaries for the "Dineh" on this earth.

He learned the importance of symbols in the life of the Navajo, who did not use the printed word. These are the means by which they expressed themselves. The ruins that were everywhere in their beloved

Canyon de Chelly were symbols of life, respected and held sacred. Every plant was a symbol of life in the Navajo mythology, all plants to be revered. "Child of white corn am I, there I wander . . . on the trail marked with pollen may I travel. . . ." It was in all their prayers, said the medicine men, in all their ceremonies. The symbols were in their sandpaintings in the colors black, blue, yellow, and white. The Emergence of the People was first from the Black World, the beginning of time; then to the Second World, the color changing to blue, the beginning of life; into the Third World, yellow, the organization of people, the sense of community; and finally, today's world, white, the glittering world, the world according to Blessingway.

Carl began to understand from the medicine men and women, who had spent a lifetime learning and performing the ceremonies, the nature of the Navajo belief in a Supreme Being. The symbols and the expression of this great unknown power were everywhere, in all creation. From as far back as Navajos remembered, they believed that the Divine Spirit was to be found in all things of the world, great and small, in the daily things around one. They believed that man, animal, plants, Mother Earth, Father Sun, the moon, the stars, and all physical bodies had the essence of this great power within them.

They believed it was this spirit, this "indwelling intelligent life," within each thing that makes it what it is. Each is an expression of thought that forms from the mind of the Creator. Each is said to have its own song, its own vibration, and these must work together in harmony, if the good within each is to triumph over the evil. In the Navajo way of life, harmony, beauty, and happiness are all interrelated. They are the source of mental and physical health in man. For the Navajos, living in harmony with nature means being fully aware of the joys, the beauty, the fullness of life, and accepting the hardships of their daily existence. And always, each Navajo feels a closeness to the Mother Earth and appreciates the sacredness of the land in which he was born and the home or hogan in which he lived. His feeling for the land is a part of the complex religious philosophy that surrounds his life and gives rich meaning to it.

In the three years of the ONEO project, though it failed to produce the book on Navajo history, Carl Gorman found the guidance he needed. He was no longer drifting without a purpose, neither in his life, nor in his knowledge of what it meant to be a Navajo. He had gained a profound awareness for people who lived in the past. It was less a matter of factual data—dates are often ambiguous in Navajo history—as it was a growing consciousness of the many passages his people had gone through in order to survive. Now Carl had a new confidence in himself, a new sense of his own continuity in the total Navajo scene, past or present. From this time on, at home or with "outsiders," he felt qualified to interpret his Navajo culture in an articulate way. When the time came for him to act on a broader scene, he was ready.

Waiting to Be Fed. 1982. Watercolor. 24 × 18 inches.

Birth of Changing Woman. 1970s. Oil on canvas. 36 × 24 inches.

Four Holy People. 1970s. Acrylic on plyboard. 18 × 24 inches. Collection of
Robert Benjamin, Albuquerque, New Mexico.

Chumash Rock Painting. 1972. Acrylic on plyboard. 32 × 24 inches.

Bear Dance. 1977. Lithograph. 36 × 24 inches. Collection of the Heard
Museum, Phoenix, Arizona.

Untitled. 1982. Watercolor. 20 × 14 inches.

Gossip. 1982. Watercolor. 20 × 14 inches.

Untitled. 1983. Acrylic on canvas. 30 × 24 inches.

FOURTEEN

Early in 1970, not long after the ONEO project was terminated, Carl Gorman received a telephone call that changed his life immeasurably and took him away from the reservation for more than three years. The call came from Professor Jack D. Forbes, head of the native American studies program at the University of California at Davis. He wished Carl to come there to teach Indian art. He sincerely felt, he said, that Carl's presence at Davis, his knowledge, and his art would be extremely important to the program. It was already the beginning of the winter session. Carl would have to come as soon as possible, within a matter of days.

Jack Forbes and the Gormans had known each other for a long time. They first met ten years before when he was a professor in the history department at San Fernando State College. There had been an interview with Forbes in the local Northridge paper about a book of his, *Apache, Navajo and Spaniard*, published in 1960 by the University of Oklahoma Press. Intrigued with the article, Carl decided there were things in the book he wanted to talk to the author about, and he and Mary arranged to go and see Forbes. They found him a charming, articulate man in his forties, with a deep personal interest in Indian problems, outspoken on the need to recognize the right of all the Indians of this country. He had grown up in the East and was proud of the fact that he had Indian (Powhatan) blood. Dr. Forbes left the college in Northridge to work with the Far West Laboratory in Berkeley, an educational group putting Indian studies together. He headed a feasibility study on the establishment of native American studies, the need for which had already been recognized

139

on at least one of the University of California campuses. Such studies were finally set up at Davis, Berkeley, and San Diego State.

On numerous occasions, Forbes discussed with Carl his concept of the school he would like to create, a university of native Americans, whose students would be enrolled from all the native peoples of America, from the Arctic to the Antarctic. For some years now he had been sending out pamphlets to interested administrators, professors, students, and businessmen in all parts of the country with the hope of getting enough interest and money to get a school like this started. He held on to the dream for a long time.

Forbes had gone to Davis as a professor in the anthropology department. For administrative reasons, the native American studies program was set up within the department of applied behavioral sciences. Coordinating this work with him, on the faculty as a lecturer was David Risling, Jr., from the Hupa Tribe, who was then chairman of the California Indian Education Association. The new program, known as Tecumseh Center, was staffed with scholars, artists, and people experienced in Indian affairs and Indian community development. Courses were concerned with the heritage of native Americans, their culture, and their art, with American history and traditional academic courses viewed from an Indian perspective. The program was open to both Indian and non-Indian students.

During the 1960s, there was a growing impetus to recognize the status of the American Indians, to emphasize the need for giving them fuller advantages and opportunities for education.

Carl had come to Davis in June of 1969, at Forbes's request, to participate in an organizational meeting for the native American studies program which would begin that fall. He liked the prospect of going to Davis in a full-time position that winter, and he accepted at once. He and Mary had less than a week to pack everything and get to Davis. They set out in their station wagon, jammed to the roof, a loaded U-Haul trailer behind. Six-year-old Zonnie was squeezed into a small open corner of the back seat. They drove through the Mojave Desert at night, arriving at Davis in northern California late the next day. There, Dr. Forbes had a small apartment waiting for them.

The native American studies program at that time was set up in Tecumseh Center, a two-story former army barracks on the campus. Three offices were downstairs, and a large student room with a kitchen attached. Carl had his workshop upstairs. All academic classes were held in classrooms on the campus. The first course that Carl Gorman taught was "Indian Art in Cultural Perspective, with Workshop." At Tecumseh Center, Carl gathered a few Indian artifacts and set them up in a room. Interest was aroused, and more things were brought in, loaned, and donated by students, faculty, and friends. Soon several rooms were needed for the collection of paintings, weavings, children's art, jewelry, pottery, Indian posters, and native costumes. Someone had put Carl's name on the door, and from early on, the students always called this place the Carl N. Gorman museum.

At the beginning of the second semester, in addition to his art course, Carl was asked by Dr. Forbes to teach Navajo history and culture, too. Many of the California Indians who were students at Davis had no knowledge of or concern for Indian history and culture in general, or for their own in particular. Perhaps Carl could help them come to a new awareness of their Indian heritage. In an interview with the press, Forbes said,

> From our viewpoint, Carl Gorman is as significant for other skills as he is for his individual art work. His years of experience as Director of the Navajo Arts and Crafts Guild and as Director of the Navajo Cultural project have given him a background in these areas that we badly need. Our primary interest in Indian studies is not so much in the training of individual artists as it is in the community development approach to arts and crafts. . . . Thus, Carl Gorman as an experienced artist, manager, and historian, brings a set of skills which we greatly need and which are quite rare combined in the same person. . . .

These were the turbulent years when universities were full of dissenting students, when anti-Vietnam rallies disturbed campuses across the country. Youth was in rebellion. It was a period when Indians, too, began asserting their own rights, demanding self-determination. It was the time of the Indian occupation of Alcatraz in San Francisco Bay, of mounting feelings of hostility. Carl was deeply involved with his students and sympathetic with their goals. He had been a rebel himself in his youth, and he still thought of himself as one in his opposition to racism and injustice. He understood the militancy of his Indian students. They would come to him after class hours talking excitedly about their problems, about the prejudice and the fearful backlash that was taking place. In the role of mentor, he felt it important to advise a course of sanity in this chaotic scene. Militancy was all right, he would say to them. It woke people up, brought attention to terrible problems that existed. "But you have to be careful with it," he said. "If you keep it up too long, there's a great danger that you will defeat yourself, you will destroy what you set out to do." The students could see that he had been tested by time, that he understood the nature of rebellion, that he had been part of it. They understood what he meant, and they listened to him as one who knew firsthand of the ordeals Indians had suffered from others.

There was almost no violence on the part of Indians at Davis. The students began to turn their emotions away from the Vietnam War, and toward their own Indian goals of rights, of recognition, of national respect.

At U. C. Davis, Carl Gorman began to paint again, after four long years. He said later that his California Indian students were responsible for accomplishing the feat. One of them, a young geologist, brought in photographs of early Chumash Indian rock paintings which he had taken in Southern California. Others had studied Campbell Grant's work on Chumash paintings. In class, as they worked on their own interpretations, some asked Carl to demonstrate how he would do it. They finally broke him down, and he at last agreed to show them. At least, he said to Mary, he could pick up a brush again without seeing Kee beside him all the time.

The rock paintings of the Chumash recalled to Carl Gorman the pictographs on the canyon cliffs he loved to copy as a child. It wasn't long before he began to work at capturing the Chumash cave paintings on canvas for himself. In the strength and complexity of their symbolism, he found an inner excitement again, a flow of creative energy he had not felt in a long time.

For Mary, the three years at Davis were a rich period. She was thrilled with Carl's position at Davis, with his renewed enthusiasm and his love of teaching. People she met on campus told her that he was a great teacher. She was also thrilled with the unexpected and exciting realization that he was starting to paint again. And she found satisfying the acceptance of him as an Indian and of her as his wife, in university activities, in social functions.

Often by herself when Carl was occupied with his work, Mary attended student meetings with other faculty wives. She was on an ad-hoc committee to deal with ethnic studies in the public schools of Davis. It was important to Mary that she and Carl were making a contribution, not only to the awakening of Indian students but to the community at large. When Carl prepared his lectures—and soon, when he was asked to present papers—Mary was his critic, consultant, rewrite editor. She spent many hours in the Davis public library doing research on California Indians and on the students and culture Carl was dealing with here. She went over Carl's work with him, encouraging him to put his thoughts down on paper clearly, in the same easy, natural style he used on the platform.

The Gormans' daughter, Zonnie, a beautiful child of eight, was already proficient in several Indian dances, including the intricate Hoop Dance. She loved to perform, dancing for adult groups, as well as in her elementary school in Davis. Zonnie made friends with the children at school easily; she was open about her emotions.

Zonnie with her father, St. Michael's, Arizona, 1968.

When she was in the fourth grade, Zonnie came home one afternoon in a total rage. She blurted out her story to Mary. While the regular teacher was tutoring a child, a young black student teacher had taken over. She was reading from a book about Indians, Zonnie said, and then she asked if anyone knew what a reservation was. Everyone in the class nudged Zonnie to answer, so she spoke up and explained about a reservation, what it was like, how big it was. The teacher looked hard at her and asked Zonnie how did she know, did her father work there? "I just said I was a Navajo and I was raised on a reservation," Zonnie said. "The teacher was real angry at me for saying that. She said I was lying. She said I was a Chicano—why did I lie about it?"

"Did you say anything then?" Mary asked.

"No. I went and found my regular teacher and told her about it. She explained to the new teacher I was really a Navajo. She still refused to believe it. So we all went to the principal's office, where the secretary just said I was Carl Gorman's daughter."

That was the end of it, according to Zonnie, because everyone on campus knew who Carl Gorman was. "And all the kids were proud of me," she said by way of conclusion. What clearly emerged from the episode and Zonnie's telling of it was her security in her own identity. Mary told her husband the whole story that night. "Good for Zonnie," was his comment. "I guess we haven't done such a bad job of bringing her up after all."

Dr. Forbes was pleased and encouraged by the success of his Indian studies program at Davis. With the help of Carl Gorman, David Risling, Jr., and their associate, Ken Martin, he prepared a book on setting up similar programs in Indian curricula. *A Handbook of Native American Studies and Chronology of Native American History*, published by the University of California Press in 1971, became the prototype for such departments in many other universities.

Meanwhile, Forbes was still determined to carry out his dream of starting a university for native Americans in which the students could work toward a degree. The dream became possible in 1970 when Dr. Forbes was given the backing of the California Indian Education Association, a strong statewide organization. He also received considerable support from the large, politically well-organized Chicano community. The name chosen for the new school was D.Q.U., Deganawidah-Quetzalcoatl University; Deganawidah (founder of the Iroquois Federation) and Quetzalcoatl (an Aztec diety) represent the native American and Chicano involvement respectively.

A former army communications center, seven miles west of Davis, was declared surplus property by the government at this time. It was a splendid site for the proposed university, a square mile in size, with a number of large buildings suitable for dormitories, lecture halls, offices, and classrooms. On behalf of D.Q.U. Dr. Forbes, David Risling, and others immediately applied for the site to the U.S. Department of Health, Education, and Welfare. Others applied too, including the University of California at Davis, which wanted to move and expand its existing primate research project.

Indian and Chicano students from Davis and nearby colleges decided there had been too much delay, and they took action. More than sixty of them went over the protective fence one night and occupied the depot. Meanwhile, the leaders of D.Q.U. began a court action to halt the projected transfer of the title to U. C. Davis. The university finally withdrew its own application. In April 1971, the deed to the site was officially transferred by HEW to the D.Q.U. board of directors.

The new university was chartered as an open school for anybody, though the students were primarily Indians and Chicanos. Professors from Davis volunteered their time to teach classes. Carl Gorman came regularly to teach the Navajo language. Dr. Forbes was certain that when

144

D.Q.U. was thoroughly established, he would launch other programs that he wanted—in economic development, nursing, and health—like those in a good community college. After a period of time, most of the Chicanos dropped out. D.Q.U. finally became an all-Indian university. (As of this writing, D.Q.U. is still functioning, with a student body of one hundred and sixteen. The school is run entirely by Indians. In 1978, it was accredited as a two-year college by the Western Association of Colleges.)

Carl Gorman's activities took him beyond the Davis Campus and D.Q.U. Before long, the word had spread that he was an excellent lecturer, an Indian with solid ideas and a fresh way of speaking them. He received a call from Chaplain Dale Heckman of the University of the Pacific in Stockton, asking Carl if he would like to speak on the subject, "What Indians Are Thankful for on Thanksgiving Day."

Carl thought it a very funny suggestion, to an Indian. But they were thankful, he said, and that's how they lived every day. The chaplain changed his request. He suggested Carl speak on material from his lectures at Davis, called the "Navajo's Vision of Earth and Man." Would he be willing to come to the university in Stockton and give his talk? "The Navajos," he said, "have a lesson for people today."

Carl began to realize the scope of the subject he had agreed to. How did one condense all that history, religion, and philosophy down to one speech, with so little time to do it? Mary helped him. They sat up all night together, working on it, then they drove the seventy-five miles to Stockton, and Carl gave the lecture, his "Thanksgiving Day speech," to an Anglo community audience. The people were enchanted by this broad-shouldered Navajo in his sixties, who dramatically presented the depth, variety, and richness of his Indian religion and culture, tying its philosophy with relevance to the present, simply and clearly.

After the lecture, the Gormans drove to Window Rock for their own Thanksgiving dinner with Carl's half-sister and her husband, Joe Watson, Jr., who worked with the Presbyterian church. He was impressed with the lecture Carl had given and took their typewritten version back with him to New York. "A New Vision of Earth and Man" was first printed in the Presbyterian ministerial publication *Monday Morning*, and later reprinted widely. A few weeks after his lecture, Carl received a phone call from the Division of Mass Media of the United Presbyterian church in New York. They wanted to make a film on the subject based on the material in his lecture. They were certain, they said, that such a film would promote understanding between white people and Indians and help improve racial relations, and they would put up the money for it. Carl said it was fine with him. Immediately they flew out from the East with a film crew. The finished film, *In Beauty I Walk*, presented Carl and his Navajo philosophy of life and, interwoven through it all, a warm portrayal of the Navajo land and its people. Completed in October of 1972, it was distributed through the United Presbyterian Film Centers to schools, colleges, and churches throughout the country.

Churches continued to ask Carl if he would lecture to their congregations, virtually always with a preface to their request that his kind of presentation and his thoughts about native culture could "bring a better understanding to them all." Typical of the notices in the press was one in the Davis *Enterprise*, dated May 5, 1972, "Navajo Instructor to Speak at Community Church Service":

> The Davis Community Church has announced that Carl Gorman will be the guest speaker at the church's 6:30 contemporary service this Sunday.
>
> Gorman is an instructor in Navajo language, art, music, and religion at U.C. Davis and D.Q.U. As Gorman speaks about "A New Vision of Earth and Man," he will take participants on a journey on the deserts and canyon lands of the Southwest where people have a life of reverence for the earth between the Four Sacred Mountains.
>
> This is an opportunity for all Christians and other people to get a glimpse into the life and religion of the Navajo people and to learn how the church can relate to the American Indians in a just way.

Wherever Carl Gorman lectured now, his audience of teachers, university faculty members, and church people found new vistas opening up to them. They were amazed to discover that Navajo Indians had a full-bodied religion, with complex, detailed stories of the Creation and a belief in a Supreme Being. Several ministers compared it, in many respects, to their own Bible.

Through Carl, the Navajos were revealed as people with an ancient and treasured way of life, a philosophy by which they lived, a positive approach that had allowed them to survive over the centuries. "Our thoughts weave all things together in the fabric of life," Carl Gorman pointed out. "We believe in the power of thought, that everything originates in thought, that it is the force that forms our lives. It is perhaps the root substance of Creation, coming from the mind of the Great Unknown Power." He explained the Navajo Blessingway, defining the importance of the ceremony in the lives of his own people, how it reinforced them with the retelling of the heroic myths, how it was there to overcome evil, to restore harmony in their lives, so that they might walk the "corn pollen path of beauty."

Carl Gorman's stay at U. C. Davis was coming to an end. After three and a half extremely busy, productive years, he was leaving to go back to the Navajo reservation in a new position. He and Mary had spent

Carl with portrait of his father, U.C. Davis, 1971.

long hours with many of his young students who needed support in this difficult period, who were questioning the values of modern civilization. They were worried about the ecology, about the threat to life from nuclear energy. He saw them turning toward the ideas of native Americans. "They're listening," he said to Mary as they prepared for departure. "The students really seem eager to learn from us. They see that Indians have a reverence for life, that we have an old knowledge that can help mankind to survive. Maybe we've done some good here," he said as he was packing his books, his art supplies. "At least, I have some hope we're all beginning to come together."

Carl could have stayed on at Davis for another year or two—retirement age was sixty-seven. But he was summoned by the new Navajo Health Authority to be their director of native healing science. Working with both American medical doctors and Navajo medicine men, he would be coordinating the time-tested Navajo healing sciences—their use of native herbs, diagnoses, and ceremonies—with the modern treatments and cures of western medicine.

His leaving U. C. Davis was the occasion for tribute. First, the museum he had been in charge of was officially dedicated as the Carl N. Gorman Museum. When Carl heard about this, he was amused. "I always thought they named museums for people when they were dead," he said, "and here I am. I'm still alive."

Over two hundred faculty members, students, and close friends came as invited guests to the dinner celebration for the new museum, in Carl's honor, held in the nearby silo building. The speeches of the evening were warm with praise. There was high tribute from Jack Forbes, who had brought him to Davis. Carl was awarded four eagle feathers for his service in the formative years of the UCD native American studies program by program coordinator David Risling. He gave credit to Carl for helping build one of the best programs of its kind in the nation; perhaps, most of all, Carl had meant so much to the staff, he said, to all the faculty and students at Davis, because he was "in all things a fully functioning, feeling human being."

Carl thanked him for his compliments and the crowd for their applause. Mostly, he said, he had wanted his Indian students to know their heritage. Many younger Indians today were urban Indians, not raised on the reservations, and they resented the white dominant culture and its pressures. But knowing their own culture and taking pride in it would give them a good foundation. It was something to hold on to when things got rough. "Maybe the best way to end," he said, "is to remember when I talked to some of the students at first. They didn't want to say they were Indians. Or they didn't know anything about their culture. But when they got involved in learning about their people, when they got started in rock paintings, or language, or native dances and music, or whatever, they became more interested and they wanted to know more. And that was good."

He said goodbye to his friends. He told them how much he had enjoyed being with all of them, working with them. Now he had new work to do. With Mary and Zonnie, he was going back to Window Rock again.

FIFTEEN

The Gormans were coming home. The headlights of their station wagon picked up the sign that pointed toward Window Rock. They turned off the freeway and headed upward to the Navajo land.

Carl opened the window of the car. A light rain was beginning to fall, the soft "she-rain" that nourished and comforted the land. He felt alive in the presence of the rain, its surrounding presence, as he never had when in California and its cities. The rain was not something beyond himself, falling "out there," a separate element. It was part of the total house of nature in which he was dwelling once again. All day that feeling had grown within him. He had come in early morning from the "House Made of Dawn." He had reached through the mounting hours to the "House of Sun-Goes-Down." Now he was moving gently into the "House of Falling Rain." As they rode through the Navajo night, Carl was once again in harmony with the rain that was part of the earth, born of it and returning to it; he and his family were total participants, sharing its beauty, its essence.

The next morning he went to work. The Navajo Health Authority was housed in a group of white trailer buildings almost diagonally across the highway from the trailer home where the Gormans now lived in St. Michael's, three miles west of Window Rock. Carl's office was in a corner section looking out toward the pines of Ganado Ridge. This was his headquarters for the next three years. He soon became aware of how limited his knowledge of Navajo medicine had been. In the experience with ONEO, he had concentrated his attention on the history and the religion of his people, seeing the correlation of the two. Now he was finding out each day more about the Navajo art of healing, how complex it was, how inextricably their religion and medicine were one.

Carl's job involved two main tasks. One was to compile a complete catalogue of Navajo herbs and plants: the hundreds that had been used by their practitioners over the centuries for specific illnesses and ailments. The second was to hold discussions with medicine men, with the aim of getting them to work together and become an organized group interacting more with the Anglo doctors on the reservation. There was need for both, in treating their people, he said. It was a good time to bind together the Navajo way of curing and the white man's way of treating illness.

The concept was valid and rational, but the human problem was there. One problem was altering the mind-set of highly traditional medicine men. Just as difficult was trying to change the attitude of the typical American physician. Carl came home one night to his trailer home, bursting with anger. An Anglo doctor at Fort Defiance hospital had become hostile, challenging Carl, mocking him for his "absurd" ideas about medicine. Carl had blown up, telling the doctor he was a "damn pill-pusher" and ought to start treating people the way the Navajos did, treating their whole being as well as their body, the way the Navajo medicine men did! "What did he say?" Mary asked. Carl's anger began to subside. He shook his head. "The fellow walked out on me," he said.

Carl Gorman's work took on a new direction. His role became increasingly that of teacher, educator, communicator. He saw the importance of presenting to Anglo medicine and to the community at large the valid contributions of Navajo medicine and its practitioners. He wanted to clear away the ignorance, the misunderstandings from which prejudice and intolerance flowed. He gave interviews to newspapers and magazines and on television. As the publicity increased, he was invited to speak at medical schools, first in the Southwest, then at universities as far away as Michigan, Texas, Massachusetts, and Washington. Each time, he came back impressed with the fact that the students listened to what he had to say. They would come around afterwards, full of questions, curious for the truth. He made it clear that the Navajo medicine man was a learned practitioner concerned with healing, who was trusted by his people and was important to their well-being. The total life of the patient was his care. For a Navajo to be sick meant that he was "broken" or "fragmented." If a patient was to be cured of his illness, whatever it was, he had to be helped to be whole again. Then he would be a complete person, in harmony with nature, with his family and friends, and most of all with himself.

Wasn't this, Carl Gorman reasoned, what advanced men of medicine were talking about, in their concern that a great proportion of all physical

150

Herbalist Sonacee Nez and Carl at tape recorder,
St. Michael's, 1975.

illnesses stemmed from mental or emotional problems? Weren't many
of them saying how vital it was to have a "total approach" to the patient,
including the psychological and social needs, his family and even his
friends in treating his illness? But this was what the Navajo medicine
men had been practicing for hundreds, perhaps thousands of years, Carl
reminded his audiences. They had seen it work. In their positive, supportive approach, everything in the ceremony they performed—the retelling of the heroic tales, the chants, the herbs or medication they
used—all reinforced their patient, to lead him into a positive way of
thinking to a strong inner feeling that he could be cured. Never under-
estimated was the role of the family and clan members, who arranged
the healing "sing," helping with their donations of money, sheep, provisions. By their total support, they would speed the recovery of the
patient. Also, and this was significant, they were sustained and strengthened themselves in the process. In the Navajo ceremonial, the healing
for one was for everyone there as well.

Carl Gorman's hopes of innovation, of high accomplishment at
home in the medical area were unfulfilled. The Navajos are not easily
propelled into new endeavors or relationships. Over the decades, they
have adapted and survived, absorbing ideas, reflecting upon changes,
taking the good as they come to see it. But in the short run, for one who
wants to see things quickly changed with the "Dineh," the likelihood

is that he will be destined for frustration while time passes, while people ponder, argue, reject, set aside decision making. Carl found numerous obstacles in his way when he tried to convince the medicine men of the need to come together, of the value of working closely with the Anglo medical people. It was a very different experience from the one he had with the small advisory board of medicine men in the ONEO project, where they all had a common goal in their quest for Navajo history and lore. Here there was conflict. There were well over five hundred Hataathlii, diagnosticians, herbalists scattered over the reservation, respected in their own regions or communities, devoted to the practice of their chosen profession. Each was a person who occupied a position of strength in his own right. Carl met with resistance on traditional grounds, with personal opposition to him as an intruder, with sheer, disdainful rejection of his plans. Moreover, in the Navajo Health Authority new executive personnel came in. Politically oriented, they could not agree with Carl in his desire to bring traditional medicine into a working relationship with modern Anglo treatments. Even the compilation of his almost completed book-catalogue on Navajo herbs and plants was held up—for "the time being," it was said.

Carl had been through this kind of thing before. Something was begun that was not to be finished. He was sure it would happen again. He could still laugh and say, "That's the way those Navajos are," meaning himself, too. But if you were going to survive, you had to be flexible, accept whatever came to your path of life, the way the old ones accepted the thunder and the lightning, the fierce storms and droughts, the hunger and thirst, the injustices of mankind, the blows of fate. You brought your thoughts around to those things that still would continue to be, the loveliness of the land, the comfort in your prayers at dawn, the joy and closeness of family and friends, the love and respect of people in your own community.

A man's role in the Navajo world can take many forms. An old friend of Carl Gorman's, a clan brother who had been his student companion and advisor fifty years ago in the Albuquerque Indian School days, called from Crystal one day to say that his eldest daughter was getting married. He wanted Carl to officiate at the wedding. Among the Navajos, a friend of the family and one acquainted with the traditions of the ceremony was qualified to perform the service.

On a warm August day a week later, Carl and Mary stopped at the FedMart in Window Rock to buy a present. The huge, paved parking lot of the shopping center was jammed with row upon row of pickup trucks, red, white, brown and buff, blue and white—the omnipresent vehicle of today's Navajo. Kids were everywhere, packages of potato chips or cans of soda pop in their hands. Many of the drivers of the pickup trucks were Navajo women, some young in modern garb, many middle-aged and dressed in their traditional velvet blouses and full skirts, wearing their beautiful Navajo silver and turquoise bracelets, concho belts, squash-blossom necklaces. A young girl in blue jeans, her hair up in big pink rollers, got out of a pickup truck. She carried a baby wrapped securely in a Navajo cradleboard. This blending of the old and the new was inherent in the Navajo way, which is to accept a changing pattern of life, to adapt to it and enjoy the advantages. Driving scores of miles in a swift truck to a great modern market has replaced the long trek by wagon or on foot to a regional trading post. Wearing the century-old mode of dress and the traditional jewelry, the Navajo woman pushed a shining metal cart through the aisles of a teeming FedMart.

The interior of the vast market was a hectic scene. As Carl and Mary entered, long lines were already stretching out behind the half dozen checkstands. Shopping carts were piled high with provisions of an infinite variety—new jeans and cellophane-wrapped shirts, toys and hair spray, six-packs of Pepsi Cola, quarts of oil, cans of kerosene, packages of meat, and bags of apples. There were items for the old and the young, all at reasonable, sometimes bargain prices, and without the addition of federal tax, a fringe benefit for living on the reservation. Some aisles of the market were narrow canyons, towering on both sides with cartons of canned and packaged foods. Other aisles were avenues of indulgence, small children sitting on the floor by great racks of comic books, poring over the colored pages. Navajo adolescents, lolling by the long stands of records and cassettes, examined the latest issue from the world of music. Among the modern electrical gadgets and appliances, waffle irons, toasters, and hair dryers, several elderly Navajo women in traditional dress, their faces wrinkled by years of exposure to wind and sun, were studying the items as they conversed in Navajo.

Mary picked out a casserole for the bride and groom, something they could use when they moved into their new home. Carl came by with the customary wedding present, a large sack of flour.

They left the supermarket and drove northward toward Crystal. On their right, the soaring rock formations were a burnished red in the late afternoon light. Bands of tall pine grew splendidly upward from the seemingly barren rock. Soon the Gormans came to a small wooden sign on a fence post by the roadside. It read "Crystal—5 mi.," and Carl turned onto a narrow paved road. The fields all around were a sea of soft beige and gold. A pair of baldheaded turkey vultures wheeled upward and away, consummately beautiful in their effortless, rolling flight. Three raucous silk-black ravens dropped out of the sky and pecked voraciously at a hunk of carrion on the roadside. On a rough-hewn fence post, a small mountain bluebird lighted for a moment before taking off. Up ahead, the Chuska Mountains suddenly emerged, heavy with thick stands of tall ponderosa pine. A dirt road took the Gormans away from the paved highway that curved up through the mountain pass. They passed the little community of Crystal, with its trading post, white church, and scattered cottages, and they reached a lightly wooded area where the wedding hogan was situated. A half dozen pickup trucks were parked nearby in the open field, a few horses tethered beyond. Families were arriving, the women casually dressed or in traditional Navajo skirts and velvet blouses; some men wore sports shirts, some colorful velvet ones, even more adorned with silver than the women. Carl Gorman took off his heavy brown jacket as he got out of the station wagon. His shirt was a golden velvet. He pulled his concho belt tight, brushed the silver sections with his sleeve to bring out their glint. He drew a square head scarf from his pocket, light brown with flower decorations, folded it carefully into a narrow band, then bound it around his forehead. He tied a large knot on the side with a flourish, turning to Mary for approval.

The hogan was packed with young people and old, standing against the walls, seated on the floor, laughing, talking, waiting for the ceremony to begin. Carl Gorman remained near the open doorway. A floor space against the rear wall was ready for the wedding party, covered with lovely Crystal rugs of the region, warm earth colors and simple geometric designs. Old Navajo rugs were hung on the wall behind them. Sitting on opposite sides of the rugs were two older Navajo couples. Those on the left were the parents of the bride; the other two were the groom's. They were quiet, unsmiling. The crowd noises dropped down as the bride and groom came through the doorway. They were in their early thirties and traditionally dressed. She was a secretary at the Navajo Community College; he worked in the finance department, Navajo Tribal Affairs, as a computer programmer.

The bride came forward, the groom beside her. She held a shallow coiled willow basket in her two hands. The two sat down on the floor between their parents. The bride leaned forward and put the basket on the floor in front of them. This was the traditional wedding basket, filled with ground corn meal, a symbol of fertility, which the bride had cooked and prepared herself. For the Navajos, corn meal is the "staff of life."

Carl Gorman approached and knelt down before the wedding basket, his head bent over it. He drew a pouch from his side pocket, sprinkled corn pollen over the basket. He said no words, uttered no prayers. He was blessing the basket and the ceremony with the corn pollen, putting it first in the center. The cross, where all lines came together, represented the creation of the earth. Carefully now, spilling the corn pollen gently between his fingers, Carl Gorman let it fall in four directions. The first is east to center because the Navajos believe all energy comes from the east, then south to center, west to center, north to center. The

154

lines that Carl Gorman followed with the corn pollen were said to come from the mountains and the clouds, from the four regions of the world. They were woven into the edge of the basket, representing the earth and the fertile, life-giving rain. They met in the center, the symbol of all life.

Carl Gorman rose to his feet. He was handed a woven water basket, ancient, pitch-covered. He gave the basket to the groom, who poured the water on his hands, washing them carefully, then poured the water on his bride's hands. Water was the eternal symbol, coming from the clouds, dropping to the earth, producing corn, giving all life.

A young Navajo came forward and took several flash photos of the proceedings. Nobody objected. The ritual was intimate, casual.

After they had washed their hands, the groom knelt and took a little corn mush from the center of the wedding basket. He ate of the corn mush and the bride did the same. When they finished, other members of the bridal party, first the fathers and mothers, participated in the ceremony by taking the corn mush, helping unite the couple by eating this symbol of life and fertility. An old man bent down and hungrily finished off all the remaining corn mush, scraping out every morsel from the wedding basket. Then he gave the basket to Carl Gorman, who walked over to the bridegroom's mother and presented it to her.

The groom now stood and made a formal announcement in Navajo to the assembled gathering. He was giving a present to the bride's mother because she had given her child away to him in this ceremony. His gift of a horse, some cattle, and a concho belt aroused great applause and laughter. The groom had obviously done the right thing.

The groom embraced his bride, to greater applause. But the wedding was not over. The father of the bride rose to his feet and faced the people. He spoke eloquently in Navajo, and at length, reporting how glad he was that he had such a fine son-in-law, and he hoped they would get along fine and have many children. The father of the groom equalled him in time and eloquence, affirming again and again how glad he was to have the daughter of such a family and how they would take good care of her. Others quickly came forward, elders of the community, very seriously giving advice out of their own experiences. Telling their own mistakes, they warned the couple not to make the same. A wizened old grandmother, her face tightly wrinkled from brow to chin, wished them good luck in a high, thin, sing-song voice.

Carl Gorman came close to the couple. He stood erect, eyes on the bridal couple, but the people in the hogan were his audience, too. He spoke firmly, his voice carrying with quiet authority. He reminded the couple that there was no word for wedding in the Navajo language. "A long time ago," he said to them, "the Early People called this the Planting

Ceremony, k'i'dilyé. Male and female seeds—planting equal children. The wedding basket with its symbols is to remind you of your part of the earth and the sky, of the land and all its fertility."

It was quiet in the crowded hogan as Carl Gorman went on. "This is your kind of life, your religion, your way of walking in beauty. Do not ever forget you are two people in marriage. A team, a duality. Masculine and feminine, two forces going together. Our corn, our great symbol, is both masculine and feminine. White corn for man, yellow for woman. Blessed by the Holy Ones. Our medicine man, when he collects the precious herbs, chooses from a masculine mountain, and then from a feminine mountain. He puts them together for strength." He paused for emphasis. He was the teacher now, the moralist, embracing all his audience as well as the bridal couple with his words. "Two people are meant to get along together, no matter what comes, no matter how hard the path is. You are meant to work together, plant together, exchange thoughts and feelings together. We see it happen differently in the world today. Bad things come about. But this is my advice to you. Be two people, living, working, planting together. A good team. This is the Navajo way."

When the people came out of the hogan, the sun was beginning to fall behind the blunt black peaks of the Chuskas. A clump of aspens caught the last streaming rays of the day, the turning leaves a mass of shimmering gold. The smell of good food filled the cool air. Behind the hogan, a group of women were busy around several open-pit fires, laughing, chattering, preparing the wedding feast. Huge pots were filled with mutton stew, corn, large mutton ribs. Frying pans sputtered with Navajo fried bread. A large table to one side was laden with paper plates, plastic forks and spoons, bags of potato chips, cans of 7-Up and Coca-Cola. Carl Gorman and Mary stood near the fires. Several older people came over and thanked him for his role in the ceremony. The bride's father embraced him, and the two old friends laughed continuously as they talked to each other.

A young Navajo couple approached, dressed in casual, modern clothes. The man carried a small, round-faced baby, tightly bound on a traditional cradleboard. The young woman bubbled over as she spoke to Carl, her English precise, with a high silvery inflection. Their baby had given his first laugh that morning, she said—a big happy yelp, and he was not even three months! "You must come to our Laughing Party tomorrow, Mr. Gorman," she went on, smiling, "you and your wife." Carl smiled in return. He knew there would be a traditional gathering of family and friends because the child had uttered his first laugh. The occasion was a time for rejoicing and also a "give-away" celebration, everyone getting a gift—small things, cakes, candy, pennies, and rock salt. Salt Woman, the sacred being, it was said, first gave these presents for a new baby.

At the party, the baby is helped to give a small piece of salt to each person, from a ceremonial basket. Then the baby will grow up to be unselfish, willing to share his wealth and his good luck with others. Yes, Carl said to the couple, he and Mary would be there at their baby's party.

Hungry people lined up around the women preparing food at the open fires. The flickering light and the rising smoke from the pit cast a glow over their faces as they came to have their plates filled. Carl Gorman spoke in Navajo to the trio of women who were filling his and Mary's plates with hot corn, mutton ribs, large rounds of Navajo fried bread. The women burst into uproarious laughter at what he said, and Carl joined in, enormously pleased with the effect of his words. Mary wanted to know what he had told them that was so funny, and he laughed. Those old Navajo ladies really liked a good joke, he said, especially if it was a little "dirty."

This was all a part of a good Navajo wedding, the ribald humor, the camaraderie, the outdoor fires, plentiful food and merry-making as well as the ritual and the seriousness. This was a good place for him, Carl Gorman thought. It had good memories, going back to the days when his mother grew up here in Crystal, to the workshop of his grandfather Peshlakai, and to the times he came as a child and roamed the whole place over. Carl Gorman looked up at the night sky, filled with stars, and he felt good.

In Carl Gorman's life all the facets were interwoven into the fabric of his days, each contributing its element of joy or experience to the totality of his existence. He found as much satisfaction and contentment in the comradeship of his fellow Navajos, his "brothers," as he did in his art or his teaching. He enjoyed traveling to other parts of the country when he was invited to lecture, participating in another community and feeling that wherever he went, he was bringing his own world with him.

He was excited on returning home from the wedding in Crystal to hear that the Navajo Code Talkers who had developed the secret code for the Marine Corps had been invited to march in the Pasadena Rose Bowl Parade on New Year's Day 1975, along with the Navajo Tribal Band. This was a special honor and a trip Carl and Mary would not miss.

For almost a quarter of a century after the end of World War II, the contribution of the Code Talkers had been virtually unknown to most Americans. "We were considered the best kept secret of the war," Carl Gorman said later in an interview with the *Pendleton Scout*, a Marine Corps publication.

"No one knew of our existence. In fact, it was long after the war that most of our own Marines finally heard of us." Part of the reason was that the Code Talkers themselves, as well as the Marine Corps, kept their work a secret because of its value, if there were to be another war. Then the highly sophisticated communication equipment used in Korea made the secret unnecessary.

The time had come for recognition. Each year at its annual reunion, the Marine Corps Fourth Division, "The Fighting Fourth," had honored a commanding officer or a distinguished combat hero. In 1969, at the recommendation of Lee Cannon, press secretary for the Fourth Division, who knew the accomplishments of the Navajo Code Talkers, the decision was made to honor them as a group. Of the more than four hundred qualified Code Talkers, fifteen were found from the Fourth Marine Division and one each from the First, Second, Third, Fifth, and Sixth to attend the reunion in Chicago on June 28, 1969. Among them was Carl Gorman, from the Second. They were flown there by transport plane. Marines were assigned to them as special hosts. They took part in a memorable parade through the streets of downtown Chicago. The final honor came at the reunion banquet in the Sheraton Hotel, where high-ranking Marine Corps officers presented the Code Talkers with a specially minted medallion in commemoration of their distinguished service.

Within the next two years, the Code Talkers Association of the Marines was formed. This was primarily at the instigation of Lee Cannon and Martin Link, the director of the Navajo Tribal Museum, who gave them space to meet in the museum and whose help and guidance were invaluable. Both Anglos, they felt the organization would not only be a valuable group for the Navajo men, but it would awaken a spirit of pride

Mary, Marine Corps General P. X. Kelley, Carl, Mrs. Kelley, on the occasion of the Fourth Marine Division honoring Navajo Code Talkers, Naval Officers' Club, Long Beach, California, 1975.

Code Talkers on parade, Gallup, New Mexico, 1979.

in the Navajo nation for what they had accomplished. Sixty Code Talkers attended the first reunion at Window Rock in July 1971. They reminisced about their war experiences. On a hill above the tribal museum, they put on an exhibition of code talking, as it was done during the war, with radios provided by the Marine Corps. Two stations were set up a half mile apart and messages in Navajo code were sent back and forth. "We realized," Carl Gorman said, "how we helped shorten the war with our language." He had come down from U. C. Davis where he was teaching. He was asked to be the first president of the association. He declined because he felt his position at Davis would keep him too far away, but he agreed to be the representative of the Second Marine Division.

In the years that followed, although most of the men were scattered throughout the reservation and there were difficulties in getting together, the idea grew of taking part in public affairs, of being seen in public. After their participation in the Rose Bowl Parade of 1975, they were asked to march as a group in many other parades. They were proud

Carl speaking at National Code Talkers' Day, Red Rock State Park, New Mexico, 1982.

of their appearances, in their bright new Code Talker uniforms of blue, turquoise overseas caps, gold-colored Navajo shirts, khaki trousers, and Navajo turquoise and heavy silver concho belts. In July 1976, at the invitation of the Bicentennial Commission, they marched in the great commemorative parade in Washington, D. C. on July 3, and in Philadelphia on July 4. The television cameras of the networks were on them.

Requests now came to the Code Talkers to take part in many public ceremonies in Flagstaff, Casa Grande, Phoenix, and the annual White Mountain Apache fair in Arizona; Albuquerque, New Mexico; and the Tuba City, Shiprock, and Window Rock fairs on the Navajo reservation. As many as twenty-five of the men would sometimes make the trip to march, paying their own way, sometimes as few as six or seven. Carl Gorman rarely failed to participate. Marching in his Code Talker uniform, he felt he was saying to the American people, "We are part of your

160

overall community, your government. We want you to see what we have done as Navajos, and that we are people who have done something to help the nation."

Throughout the Navajo land, the youth were seeing a group of their own people in a new and favorable light. The Code Talkers were examples of men who had accomplished great deeds, who were highly regarded in the public eye. Their own young Navajos looked up to them as role models. They were asked to speak at public high schools and boarding schools on the reservation. Carl Gorman was called upon often. He intrigued his audiences with his war experiences, winning them over with his description of "one hundred percent Navajo corpuscles exploding inside of me, I mean all Navajo." He always closed by discussing the importance of setting up goals for themselves as Navajos.

In the years to come, the Code Talkers continued to gain recognition. Their achievements inspired the formation of a Marine platoon of more than fifty young Navajos, whose graduation at Camp Pendleton in 1981 was to be an occasion for national publicity. In January 1982, Arizona Governor Babbitt would proclaim a Navajo Code Talkers Day in their honor. In August of that year their great contribution to the war in the South Pacific was celebrated at Red Rock State Park in Gallup, New Mexico, with high tributes from Governor King and from Chairman Peter MacDonald of the Navajo nation, and a proclamation from President Reagan, officially designating August 14, 1982 as National Navajo Code Talkers Day.

As president of the Code Talkers Association, Carl Gorman would add his personal note of tribute, singling out Lee Cannon and Martin Link, both Anglos, who had contributed so much of themselves to see that the Code Talkers were recognized, and who had helped them organize to become an important group in the lives of the Navajo people. "Without their vision and devotion," Carl concluded, "we probably still would be unknown."

SIXTEEN

The time was the spring of 1977 and Carl Gorman felt free again. His days were his own; he could go back to his studio and spend long hours again at his painting and drawing. He was sixty-nine years old, and the Navajo Health Authority had not renewed his contract, giving as their reason that he was past retirement age.

A "right path" lay ahead for him, however. He had always said there were a thousand wrong paths in life that a man could follow, but only one right one, and when a man was on that path, he would know it. An offer came to Carl to join the staff of the Navajo Community College, which he accepted at once. His position was coordinator of Navajo Resources and Research in curriculum development. He would also be a lecturer. Once more he was established in the role of educator, a role that brought him back to his home base. As a Navajo believing in Navajo ways, he would be an educator, working directly with his own young people. With a wealth of varied experience behind him, in both the Navajo and Anglo worlds, he was confident he could give them the direction and support they badly needed to face the problems in their lives ahead.

The Navajo Community College was unique, the first Indian-owned and -operated college on an Indian reservation and the first to be fully accredited. It grew out of a demand on the part of Navajo leaders for quality education for their own people. By 1957, money that was coming in from oil royalties was used to set up a scholarhip fund and send young Navajos to college. But a large percentage of the young students who received these tribal scholarships became dropouts. Many were under-educated; they needed remedial work and could not compete. Often there was insufficient planning for the special needs of the Indian student or consideration of the cultural differences between the Indian and non-Indian students.

Recognizing this need "for an institution of higher learning which could successfully bridge the cultural gap between the Navajo and the non-Indian world," the Navajo Community College was created and chartered by the Navajo Tribal Council in July 1968. The college remains owned and controlled by the Navajo Tribe. Authority for its direction is given to a ten-member board of regents. All presidents of the college, with one brief exception, have been Navajos.

In January 1969, the college held its first classes at the Bureau of Indian Affairs High School in Many Farms, Arizona. The same year, plans for a permanent campus were approved to be built on 1,200 acres of tribal lands near Tsaile, Arizona. Construction was started within two years. Classes began on the new Tsaile campus and on the Shiprock, New Mexico campus in October 1973. The college was granted accreditation by the North Central Association of Colleges and Schools in July 1976.

The purpose of the Navajo Community College was to provide a basic academic education for the students who would transfer to a four-year course, or for those who wish to complete a two-year program leading to employment in technical and vocational fields, primarily in the Navajo nation. The history, language, culture, and crafts of the Navajo and other Indian people are part of its curriculum. Navajo culture and philosophy are integrated into the teaching program "to enhance all students' respect for their unique heritage." The 1982 catalogue of the college states:

> Today more than ever before the young Navajo faces the challenge and the opportunity of dealing with two worlds, the traditional and the modern. Both are important, and he must function within both. The Navajo Nation needs professional young Navajos capable of handling the complex affairs of the modern world, using the wisdom and philosophy of the Navajo world as their foundation.

No one recognized the difficulties of such academic objectives more than Carl Gorman. He had no illusions about how much he might accomplish. But he knew he was a good teacher, that students had listened to him in the past, that there was genuine communication between him and the young people. He was content to do whatever he could in this new milieu.

Hundreds of times in the next three years, Carl Gorman was to make the long trip from his trailer home in Window Rock sixty miles northward to the Navajo Community College near Tsaile. In the wintertime, when ice or snow often covered the winding road, the trip was arduous. But when the weather was good, through most of the year, the drive was a welcome time to commune with his thoughts, to listen to the music coming from his cassette player, to move through the land he loved.

He felt much at peace on this particular August morning, looking forward to the kind of special lecturing assignment he always enjoyed. As he approached the Tsaile region, the blunt peaks of the Chuska Mountains loomed off to the right, the dark green forest of tall ponderosas opening up for him ahead. He came soon to the place where the Navajos had built their new college, at an elevation of 7,000 feet, in a large clearing with open fields around and high green woods in the background. He turned off the tape of *La Traviata.* In all these years, he thought to himself, he never seemed to get tired of hearing it.

The Navajo Community College is barely a half hour away from the sheer sandstone cliffs of Canyon de Chelly. The dormitories, the library, the dining hall, the classrooms are in the shape of the traditional Navajo hogan or home. They are octagonal and earth brown in color, designed to "reflect the strength and dignity of the Navajo culture and heritage, paralleling Navajo education with Navajo ceremonial life." The imposing, six-story Ned Hatathli Culture Center dominates the entire campus. Its entrance faces the rising sun in the east, as does the Navajo hogan. Its towering windows reflect in all four directions the deep blue sky, dotted often with white cumulus clouds. Opposite the center, a lone hogan rests in a neighboring field, a symbol of the past and present intertwined.

For two days, the college was providing a special workshop on career opportunities for Navajo itinerant workers. In his lecture this morning, Carl Gorman's task was not to tell them about their work or what to choose for a career. Others would talk about those things. His purpose and intent was to encourage them to learn more about their Navajo culture, take pride in their great heritage. He wanted them to realize how much better off they would be when they could feel this.

The large lecture hall in the cultural center was filled with over a hundred people as Carl Gorman entered. Most were young men and women dressed like students anywhere in America, in jeans and sports shirts. But a number of middle-aged people were there too; many of them women, serious and attentive, in their velvet blouses, cotton-tiered skirts, and silver jewelry.

Carl Gorman strode in to take his place in front of them on the lecture platform. He stood silent, an authoritative figure looking on his audience. The leader of the workshop program introduced him as the coordinator of Navajo resources and research, Department of Curriculum Development. It sounded impressive. He also said that Carl Gorman had been a distinguished lecturer at the University of California at Davis, on native American art and culture.

Carl Gorman raised his hand in a salute of greeting. "Yá' át' ééh, shidine'é," he called out. The group called back "Yá' át' ééh!" They leaned back, relaxed, waiting. Carl Gorman paused dramatically, his arms spread wide. "I can lecture to you in English—or," he laughed, "do you want me to talk in Navajo?"

They laughed, roaring back "Navajo!" He started to speak, warmly. He was the supreme actor onstage, holding his listeners easily as he gestured with his outstretched hands. One moment he was intensely serious, and they followed every word with the same intensity. The next, he would loosen up and smile broadly, telling one of his favorite Navajo jokes they could easily identify with. Always, on both sides, there was the quick return to earnestness as they participated in the flow of his ideas, his emotion, his fellowship.

Basically, he was saying that they no longer had to be ashamed of being Navajos or apologize for anything. His eyes glistened as he spoke. His words were firm, direct, strong. He was giving them good, practical advice. They didn't have to shrink from Anglos, he was telling them, or from any confrontation, with any fellow worker, with any employer, just because someone rebuffed them. Their ancestors never did. They were proud. They learned to accept, to go on.

"It's what I tell all my students here at the college," he said. "Navajos don't have to be afraid anymore, not the way the missionaries and the B.I.A. people made us feel. These are different times. I want to help all of you find the foundation, the strength your *own culture* gives you. Believe me, when you do, it works. We have seen it happening for a long time now, and we know it is true. People of other minority cultures have found the same truth." He paused dramatically. "I want you to think about this. You must take pride in your own culture, you must not lose your native roots. You must keep your true identity. Then you will be strong. You will be able to get along with any people, your own or any other."

Carl Gorman was fortunate at this time to have as friend and mentor the distinguished medicine man Ray Winnie, who was on the staff of the Navajo Community College as a special consultant. One department was recording his treasure of stories and legends. For another, he lectured to students on Navajo history and religion, drawing upon the myths from the ceremonies he knew. Winnie was a sturdily built, energetic man of seventy, with a youthful attitude and an immense sense of humor. His father and Carl Gorman's were from the same clan, Kin-ya-onny. The two had met during Carl's work with the Navajo Health Authority. They had a solid respect and affection for one another.

Frank Harvey (historian), Ray Clark (N.C.C. Museum staff), Carl, and Ray Winnie (medicine man) examining sacred bundles returned to Navajos from Wheelwright Museum, 1917.

Ray Winnie was a Hataathlii, highly regarded by his people. His father had been a medicine man before him. If a Navajo "singer" knew two or three ceremonies, it was considered an excellent accomplishment. Ray Winnie had mastered fifteen, including four major ones, such as the Yei-bi-chei or Nine Night Chant, the Mountain Way, the Enemy Way, the Male Shooting Way. To master any one of these takes years. He told Carl how it started for him, how one night, when he was ten, the realization came that he was blessed by the Holy People to carry out the ceremonies. It was like a vision, he said. At thirteen he went as an apprentice to a respected Hataathlii. At fifteen, he conducted a regular ceremony, and the people had respect for him. An eager student, he learned about plants and their healing qualities because it was important for him to be an herbalist also, to understand how to treat the physical side of his patient. During World War II, Ray Winnie left the reservation to work in Montana on the railroad. He associated with non-Indians, and though he never learned to speak English, he learned their ways. He said he was wiser, richer as a person, when he came back to his people. The white man's world was no longer a mystery to him, and he was not frightened by it. Now he looked ahead to the opportunity of working with the Anglo doctors, letting them see how much the medicine man with his practices could be of service in treating their Navajo patients.

Carl Gorman was meeting Ray Winnie for lunch. The two old friends strolled across the college campus. Ray Winnie walked on the ground beside the asphalt path. This way it felt right to him. His feet were close to the earth, he said. He could feel the earth; he could feel its power, its goodness.

As they approached the octagonal building which housed the cafeteria, Carl Gorman was caught up in the flow of students, Navajo boys and girls, most of them in jeans and colorful shirts. Several greeted him warmly. Most of the students were serious about their education, which was supported by the Navajo nation. They saw it was an opportunity to get ahead. They could take courses in literature, science, philosophy, and psychology. They could receive practical training to be nurses, lab technicians, emergency medical technicians. Over all, the college aimed to provide an "umbrella philosophy" of Navajo education, striving to give them deeper insight into their own Navajo way of life, their own heritage.

Carl Gorman entered the large, airy dining hall. The walls were covered with strong, stark, primitive murals painted by students in bright flat colors. The tables, well spaced, gave a sense of comfort. Ray Winnie was already in the student line, tray in hand, choosing his food. Carl Gorman followed him with his tray to a table near one of the tall windows. Several students were already seated there. How different from the way it was at U. C. Davis, Carl thought, where faculty sat in one place, separate, and the students in another. Here, they all sat together, and good talk went back and forth. They were learning from each other in a process of give and take.

The table was alive with conversation for an hour as Navajo and English went back and forth. Carl Gorman had a way of making everyone feel comfortable. Ray Winnie was the genial authority whom they loved to question. He invariably answered with long statements in Navajo, which Carl Gorman proceeded to translate in a few words, a sentence at the most. The students were concerned with the many practical problems they would have to face, above all with their need for jobs either in the present Navajo economy or off the reservation.

Carl Gorman remembered the commencement exercises the past June at the Community College where the key speaker was a beautiful young Navajo woman, who had graduated four or five years before. She had been doing graduate work outside the reservation, and now she was coming back to teach. Her speech that day was entitled "A Quest for Identity." She told the students before her and their parents and the staff clearly and forcefully that they would not find it "outside." They would find it in their own land, in themselves, in their own roots. They would find it in their family closeness, in the resources of their elders, in their native language. They would find it in the dignity and the self-esteem that came as a result of their daily quest.

Yes, these were the things they were talking about, Carl thought, as he drove home that afternoon toward Window Rock. Maybe people outside the reservation didn't understand how important it was for them to find out who they were. They were not members of a "compact majority," secure in numbers and in a solid past. They were only too conscious of the fact that they belonged to a minority, a group whose skin was of a different color, whose history had long been marked by persecution, harassment, downgrading. How could they survive in the present, they were asking, unless they could look ahead to a time when they were in control of their destinies? Their talk was of self-determination for their people, identity for themselves. These were not idle words to them. They had become symbols, a vibrant statement of their growing need to find their way in a modern society.

What was important now—and Carl felt he was part of their endeavor—was that they were thinking, they were doing, they were trying. He could see it happening with them, even as he saw it in his own home, with his daughter Zonnie.

SEVENTEEN

It was getting late. The sun was dropping, orange-gold into the horizon of white-capped August clouds, and the Gorman family was still waiting for the medicine man, Ray Winnie, to arrive so they could start out for the ceremony.

Carl Gorman was on the roof of his main trailer. Since there was extra time, he fixed the hoses of the air conditioner which had suddenly sprung a leak. He came to the edge of the roof and made his way gingerly down a ricketly brown ladder, looking toward the west. The sun had already set, but he wasn't worried. He knew Ray Winnie had to stop at a Squaw Dance on his way over, long enough to prepare the prayer stick, wrap it, fix the feathers right, give it the proper blessing.

Inside the trailer, Mary had been preparing for the ceremony. She had bought a large supply of mutton ribs. There would be at least a dozen or more people. White flour was readied for the Navajo fried bread that she and the other women were to have made before the sun went down. It would have been good, laughing and talking as they worked, sitting together, eating together. But it was too late for that now. Because of the delay, there would not be enough time to get the cooking done before the moon rose and the ceremony started. She gathered up all her Navajo silver—turquoise bracelets and earrings, necklaces set with turquoise—to be blessed by the medicine man during the proceedings.

It was Zonnie for whom the night's ceremony was to be performed. She was fifteen now, and next month Zonnie was to leave the reservation to attend a progressive Anglo private boarding school. The change of schooling had been at the insistence of R. C., her famous half brother, who adored Zonnie. "She has to expand her horizons," he said. "She must have the chance. I want her to do it, I can afford it. She has to have the right kind of stimulation for her talents. Then she can be of some real service to her people."

Carl Gorman approved. He knew it was the right path for Zonnie. She had been unhappy in the reservation schools, where they held her down. She was a talented, creative poet and dancer. She was to discover at the new school that she also possessed the family talent for art.

Zonnie herself had asked for the ceremony, out of the beautiful Blessingway. It could help her feel secure away from her family and her home surroundings, as she entered an alien environment. It would lend her strength, away from the protection of the Four Sacred Mountains and support her in following the right path during the days ahead. She believed that this would be true. She had faith in what she had learned in her home, from her father and mother both. She was proud of her Navajo heritage.

Now she was quietly waiting for the medicine man. She sat in the back room of the trailer, watching a television show, methodically working at a hooked rug, American style.

It was dark when Ray Winnie finally arrived. He pulled up to the trailer in a new white-and-tan pickup truck, opened the door and hopped down. In his mid-seventies, he was still an energetic man. He took off his broad Stetson hat to wave as he approached. Underneath he wore the traditional head scarf. A silver necklace lay heavy on his neck, a pendant turquoise suspended from it. Turquoise bracelets girded both wrists. His blue shirt was circled with a massive concho belt of old, heavy silver.

On the front seat of the pickup truck sat his wife, a slender woman, near his age, wearing a dark green velvet blouse, a full cotton-tiered skirt, many silver necklaces. She held a three-year-old grandchild in her lap. They were going to the ceremony too.

The medicine man and Carl Gorman embraced warmly. They began to talk. Neither appeared to be in any hurry. Mary Gorman and Zonnie loaded the back of their brown station wagon with provisions. The medicine man turned from Carl Gorman, nodded a greeting to them, then returned to the wheel of his truck.

They set out on the road to Ganado Ridge. The medicine man's pickup was in the lead, followed by the Gormans' station wagon. A round luminous moon was rising over the black pine trees. The ceremony could take place only on a night when the moon rose after the sun had set. It was a waxing moon, just before full.

They left the paved road behind after about five miles, turned into the thick of the tall pine woods, and followed the first road for several miles more. Finally they came into a full clearing, high on the ridge plateau. Not far away, rising up softly, were several hogans, as much a part of the earth as the dark pines beyond, all bathed in the cool white light of the moon. The Gormans left their car to greet the members of the family whose compound this was. Everyone spoke in quiet tones, as if in harmony with the night.

Carl Gorman led Mary and Zonnie into the hexagon-shaped ceremonial hogan. It was without furnishings and only a round black wood-burning stove in the center of the earth floor. A long black pipe rose up from the stove, going out through a hole in the pine-log rafters. The construction of the hogan was simple. Heavy round pine logs placed one on top of another, held together with red clay. They were simple and sturdy, warm in the winter, cool in the summer. The roof was domed, and its roundness gave a feeling of comfort and security. As they walked through the open doorway, which faces the east, they moved to the left of the stove, according to ritual, proceeding around the room from left to right. Soft, gray sheepskins were spread around the floor, against five of the six walls, for the participants to sit on. A kerosene lamp near the stove gave off a faint yellow glow. A large white sheet covered one entire section of wall.

Zonnie and her mother continued around the stove and sat down against the white sheet. The young girl wrapped a blanket tightly around her shoulders. It was cool inside the hogan.

More people came in now, including Ray Winnie's wife and grandchild, who would sit close to him. Then a half dozen men, two women, another child entered. They all took places along the walls, talking quietly, joking, several smoking cigarettes. The children soon fell asleep.

Three of the men, and the woman next to Mary, were studying to be Hataathlii medicine men. They were all apprentices. The two older men, both in their forties, had been studying for many years. On many nights, long into the night, they were learning to become healers for their people. They could study only in this way, in the presence of a traditional, highly skilled Hataathlii like Ray Winnie. There were no books, no notes to follow, no written documents. All was done by memory. It was recorded in the mind and held there, the way their people have always done, for hundreds and hundreds of years.

One of the apprentices was a boy of eighteen, just beginning. He had graduated from high school. Carl Gorman was encouraging him to go on to the Navajo Community College in Tsaile, to study to be a veterinary technician. He was also serious about studying to be a medicine man. The woman, dimly seen across the hogan in the light of the kerosene lamp, was in her late thirties. She was dressed in worn, faded blue denims and a plaid flannel shirt, the same outfit in which she had spent a backbreaking day, shearing and dipping sheep. Tonight, she leaned against the wall. She rested gratefully and waited, anticipating the ceremony.

When the medicine man, Ray Winnie, came in it was almost ten o'clock. There was no haste or urgency in his manner. He sat down against the west wall, opposite the open door. The group became silent. They looked toward him respectfully. The medicine man began to speak. The Navajo words spilled out in warm, mellow notes. He paused to light a cigarette, gingerly holding it between his thumb and forefinger. He was telling one of his stories, and the group, including Carl, listened solemnly, then laughed uproariously. It was not part of the ceremony. Ray was waiting for the moon to be exactly in the right position.

Two of the older apprentices went out and brought in wood now. They lit the fire in the stove. The faces of the men were a study in intensity as they bent before the flames.

The youngest apprentice abruptly walked out of the hogan. The medicine man set down a battered, old brown leather bag. It looked like an old-time Yankee doctor's bag. The medicine man opened it and took out a leather pouch. He extracted a small pipe, grayish-brown with age and use. He filled it with what looked like ground tobacco, "dzilth nát' oh," called "mountain tobacco." It was supposed to clear one's mind and give a positive feeling, according to Ray Winnie.

The "doctor's bag" resting beside the medicine man's chair was his paraphernalia bag. The contents had a strong, traditional meaning. They were handed down to Ray Winnie by an old medicine man, a close relative. It contained arrowheads, prayer sticks with feathers, corn pollen, herbs of different kinds, a rattle, semiprecious stones, and some shells. What Ray Winnie used depended on the type of ceremony he was performing. But as symbols of strength, they all carried the weight of ancient tradition. They were symbols of what the Navajos called spiritual continuity.

The medicine man started to chant, holding the pipe firmly in his hand. The young apprentice returned, carrying two small sticks in his hand. He was gone so long because he had to find the right ones, from the right bush. The apprentice lit the ends of the sticks at the stove fire, blowing on the tips to keep the flames alive. He carried them reverently to the medicine man, who lit the pipe with them.

Zonnie took off her moccasins at the woman apprentice's whispered request. Her bare feet rested on the gray sheepskin. She lifted her head as the medicine man chanted. She was not looking at him but staring ahead. The medicine man began very intently to inhale the tobacco smoke. He blew a short puff upward to the sky, the Father Sky, now downward to the earth, the Mother Earth. His breath and the smoke it carried embodied and invoked the spirit of life. He blew smoke on his

174

outstretched hands. He rubbed it on his feet, legs, arms, chest, and head to lend spiritual strength to his body. He continued with his chant now, passing the pipe first to Carl Gorman on his right. Carl followed the same ritual exactly, as did Zonnie, and then Mary. Everyone watched attentively as Zonnie very slowly inhaled the "smoke of life," blowing its strength above and below and upon her hands, letting its life sink into her feet, legs, arms, chest, and head. The pipe was passed to each person in the room, from left to right.

The chanting went on. The medicine man sang alone at great length, very solemnly, with continuous repetition of the same rich sounds. The rest of the group joined in, chanting solidly, an alternating solo and chorus.

Time lost all its meaning. Hours and minutes seemed suspended, past and present and future merging into one. The ancient ritual and the modern hour fused into a rich, comforting personal experience. The slow hypnotic rhythm of the chanting enveloped everyone, calming their minds, soothing their spirit and their bodies.

The singing stopped abruptly.

The two older apprentices bent down by the open stove and removed the tobacco ash from the sacred pipe. They put it into a small glass bowl and dissolved the ash with water from another glass bowl. They carried the precious contents to the medicine man. He dipped his fingers in the liquid. Then he touched his mouth, his forehead, his arms, legs, and chest. He passed the bowl to Carl. Then it went to Zonnie, to Mary, and to all the others, from left to right in the same order as the passing of the pipe. Each followed the same ritual as the medicine man. The bowl reached the men at the stove. One of them drank the remaining liquid, making certain not to leave a single drop. The "tobacco" had been brought down by Ray Winnie from one of the sacred mountains. The liquid carried its living essence, its sacredness.

This was at the heart of their religion and of their life: that the land and its gifts of plants and water, and the mountains to which they looked, were all one, alive and sacred. In the same way, all of the people were alive and sacred and one, joined that night in a simple ceremony of faith. The faces of the participants were calm and alive. No one seemed weary after their long day of work, followed by these hours at night. They appeared to gain in energy as the ceremony continued.

Long after midnight, the medicine man casually stopped chanting. He took a small pouch of corn pollen from his paraphernalia bag for the benediction. Corn pollen is a symbol of purification. The prayers, the songs were all purified and a blessing placed on the whole ceremony.

The medicine man took a little of the corn pollen between his forefinger and his thumb and he touched Zonnie with it, first, on the sole of her foot, then the knee, the hip, the chest, the shoulders, the head. Then he put some on the tip of her tongue like a priest using holy water. The ceremony for the night was over. There was no climax to the prayers, no peroration. It was simply over, an accepted part of the total day's activity. Its meaning was quietly received and accepted. The people filed clockwise around the stove, out the door, and into the white moonlight.

The medicine man said there would be a two-night ceremony instead of one. Zonnie was to remain in the ceremonial hogan during the entire day, only her mother remaining with her. The second night's ceremony would be a continuation of the first, but with different rituals, different prayers. The following morning before dawn was for the "purification" rites. Zonnie's hair was washed in yucca root suds, her body cleansed and purified with white corn meal. Behind a blanket held by the women, Ray Winnie's wife would wash her hair and rub her body with corn meal. At dawn, Zonnie would put on her best Navajo dress, a velvet blouse and satin skirt, and go outside to follow the medicine man's instructions for inhaling the life energy at sunrise. So would end the ritual for Zonnie's departure into another society. The ceremony was an expression of a support, faith, and prayer that in all the days ahead she might "walk in beauty," according to the Navajo way.

It was a simple ceremony, simple ritual. On nights like this, similar ones would take place all over the reservation with family and friends and a respected medicine man like Ray Winnie, a few apprentices perhaps. It could be a ceremony to help a troubled person, or for some illness, before an operation, or for a soldier going away or coming home. It could also be for a young person like Zonnie, preparing herself for a new adventure, going to a school or to work away from her home, her sacred land.

In the following days Carl and Mary talked with Zonnie about the ceremony. They helped her understand some of the details, the symbols and what they meant. The important thing was that she feel the message of spiritual energy from the Holy People, Carl said to her. She must know that she carried within her the continuity of life. It was the continuity of their Changing Woman, from being born, to growing old, and becoming young again. This continuity was in the change of seasons from spring to winter and back to spring. It was continuity and renewal, "sa'á nagaí k'ad bik'eh hozhǫ́."

As for the prayers and the chanting, Zonnie understood only a little Navajo, but she knew in general what they meant. She felt them. They had a special significance for her, too, because they came from the medicine man. He was the repository of the prayers and thoughts, Carl said to her, that had been handed down among their people from generation to generation.

Finally, she was supported by the group, not just by her parents, but

Zonnie performing hoop dance, Heard Museum
Indian Fair, Phoenix, Arizona, 1982.

everyone there. They gave strength to Zonnie with their prayers, the power of their thought, even as they drew new strength for themselves.

Wherever she would go, from this time on, Carl and Mary both said to her, she would remember this experience and it would sustain her. In all respects Zonnie was Navajo. She would continue to grow in strength, because the path she had chosen was a right one.

No path is easy, no matter how right it may be. In her first months away at school, far from home and the reservation and the people she knew, Zonnie went through a difficult period. There were days that were filled with loneliness, homesickness, and fear. She called her parents often, in desperate need of reassurance, and they talked long with her, giving her courage to go on.

At the end of the first semester, they received a letter from Zonnie. She started by apologizing for being so terrible those first few weeks, calling them on the phone so many times. Then, just this past week, she wrote, she was beginning to feel much better about things. She no longer felt that people thought she was different because she was Navajo.

In fact, one of her teachers encouraged her in class to talk about her people and her religion and her Navajo life. She said she was doing better now in math and in English, and one of her poems was going to be published in the school magazine. Also, she was working in clay again, doing a head like the one she had done in her dad's studio. And R. C. had written her a letter saying she could come to his studio in San Francisco during Christmas vacation, and they could work together on any sculpture she wanted to do, and he would help her.

But the best part, Zonnie wrote, was something she was really proud of. There was only one other girl in the whole school who was Indian. She was Hopi, and she had been having a hard time. She told Zonnie she wanted to quit school and go home to Oraibi. She kept saying she would never make it, everybody was against her. Zonnie told her that wasn't true. Knowing how scared the younger girl was, she made up her mind to help her, to work with her on her studies and try to keep her at school. She said she kept telling the girl she mustn't try to be like everybody else. They would respect her if she'd just be a Hopi, just be herself. When Zonnie talked to one of her instructors about the girl, he praised Zonnie for doing this and promised to find ways to help too. "Well, that's all for now," Zonnie concluded. "I thought you'd like to hear that last part. I'll write again next week. I love you, Zonnie."

EIGHTEEN

In all the active years after Carl Gorman left U. C. Davis, he painted only occasionally. He could pick up a brush again without seeing the shadow of little Kee beside him at the easel, but he produced no body of work. He was occupied with the problems of his Navajo people and with the demands made upon him as a teacher and lecturer. Mary kept urging him to go back to his painting. He was an artist, she said. It was time he went back to his art.

It was the winter of 1980. A new gallery was opening in Taos, and R. C. was helping the owner to exhibit and sponsor outstanding Indian artists from all over the Southwest. They wanted Carl to show his work, and they also asked to use one of Carl's older paintings for the exhibit's poster.

For Carl Gorman, the timing was right. He was ready, within himself. With the Taos exhibit only three months away, he had a tangible goal. He went back into his studio. He enjoyed being alone before his easel, brush in hand, a paint-spattered smock covering his large frame, the sounds of a tenor voice coming from the two stereo speakers lodged near the ceiling. He found a new security in his small trailer-studio, an artist's cluttered domain, stacked with portfolios, framed paintings, art books, and above him, the oil portrait of his father, which he had done years before, the warm burgundy color of the rancher's shirt setting off a lean, kindly face.

After many weeks, the new paintings began to appear—wild horses, herds of horses, single horses, some in color, in black on white, in white on black. The lines were strong and sparse and vital. He was going back

Carl and Mary at authors' home, Los Angeles, 1978.
Photo by Georgia Greenberg.

to what he used to do as a kid, Carl said to Mary. He worked late, forgetting to eat. She brought him a sandwich and hot coffee. The aria he listened to came to a poignant end. It was from an album of Pavarotti. Carl liked the way he sang.

Mary studied Carl's newest watercolor on the easel, a group of horses and riders on a windswept mesa, painted in stark, simple lines. It was really good, she said.

"I'm thinking differently, Mary," he said. "Drawing simpler." He wanted to get down to the basic lines, to do his horses in the fewest possible strokes, maybe a half dozen, to get at what a horse really was.

She nodded. He was doing what he loved to do, and it was coming right. This was like the old days, when he was always excited about his work, and she was his manager, and he sold almost everything he wanted to exhibit.

In April 1980, Carl and Mary went to Taos for the gallery opening. On display in the front window was Carl's original oil from which the poster was taken. It was of a still-untamed horse, tied by a huge coiled rope to a powerful stake, his tortured head upraised to the sky, his dark gray hooves frantically pawing into blue space, mouth frothing and torn, huge white teeth exposed. Carl Gorman had titled his painting *The Rope.* He said that it came out of his feelings for what men did to animals and for what other men had once done to his Navajo people.

By the end of the first evening, the gallery had sold four paintings of Carl Gorman's, including *The Rope.* The next morning the gallery

180

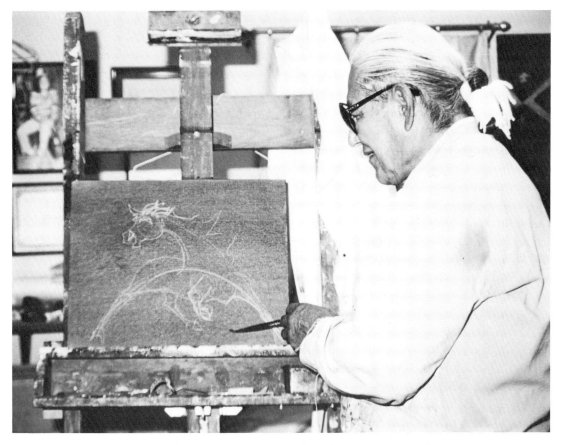

Carl in his studio, St. Michael's, Arizona, 1981. Photo by Georgia Greenberg.

held a seminar for all the artists who were exhibiting. They asked Carl to discuss with them his own ideas on native American art, what new directions he felt it should take.

Carl realized fully at this moment that his art had been the single most important thing he knew. There had been many phases, distractions, and changes in his life's direction, but he had always come back to his goal, as he came back to it now.

His role at Navajo Community College was over. He would continue to lecture to different groups throughout the country when invited, as he had done in the past. More important to him, he would continue to speak to the youth on the reservation, reminding them of the need to find strength in their culture and a goal in their life.

For himself, Carl Gorman now had the time and the desire to follow his own goal. He had the time to paint, to see emerge on his easel all the things that meant so much to him, the scenes out of his childhood, the horses, the people, the land. It was a prospect he looked forward to. It was the continuity of his life.

APPENDIX A

Excerpts from Minutes of Navajo Club Meetings

February 16, 1958. Meeting held at home of Mr. and Mrs. Peter MacDonald, 3680 W. 111th Place, Inglewood. "A letter was read that was written from Navajo Club to the Lion's Club of Inglewood—expressing appreciation for their aid to Navajo Medicine Man, Hosteeen Bihini, for operation on his eyes."

General discussion of the installation dinner and meeting. Progress was reported in securing Navajo dancers for the program. It was reported that the committee choose as its theme "From Sheepherding to Outer Space," and was planning the table decorations around this theme.

April 20, 1958. Fobes Hall, Inglewood. Installation of officers. Opened the program with Ruby MacDonald interpreting the ceremony, and Myron Denetdale portraying a medicine man. Officers installed as follows: Carl Gorman, chairman; Peter MacDonald, first vice-chairman; A So See, second vice-chairman; Myron Denetdale, treasurer; and Mary Gorman, secretary. Following the installation was a fine program of Navajo dances and songs.

May 15, 1958. Meeting held at YMCA, Fobes Hall, 315 Spruce, Inglewood. From a letter to members about recognition for Myron and Virginia Denetdale: "They were presented with a silver plaque made by Fred Peshlakai, mounted on cedar from Navajo country, cut and polished by Karl Dalton of Ganado and inscribed "Presented April, 1958 by the Navajo Club to Its Founders, Myron and Virginia Denetdale."

May 18, 1958. Chairman Carl Gorman announced the appointment of Ralph Roanhorse as Navajo tribal affairs chairman. Peter MacDonald reported that he and A So See had been invited to speak before some church group about Indians, as part of the Southern California Council of Churches Commission on Indian works program.

Sept. 21, 1958. Picnic meeting, Griffith Park. Chairman Carl Gorman. It was moved that the executive committee take up matter of inviting Mr. Paul Jones, tribal chairman, to come to speak to the club.

Nov. 16, 1958. Sunday, meeting at Inglewood YMCA to have dinner and to hear special guest speaker, Mr. Paul Jones, Navajo tribal chairman. Two selections by guest singer, Dan Eagleman, were "Pale Moon" and "Indian Love Call."

Highlights of the talk by Tribal Chairman Paul Jones were his interesting sidelights on his life and the increased duties of the tribal chairman. He told of the great responsibility falling on his shoulders and on the council members due to the new wealth and financial pressures coming to the tribe from the discovery of uranium a few years back and now the develoment of oil resources. He told of the various projects in health, education, etc. for which the tribal funds are being utilized. His talk was followed by a question-and-answer period in which he told something of the political situation on the reservation, the right of individuals to retain allotted land, inheritance rights of non-Navajos on the reservation married to Navajos, etc.

August 8, 1959. At Big Pines, San Bernardino Mountains. "Members and their families camped out for the weekend. Morris Jones delivered the sheep. The Jones, Anderson and Denetdale families butchered. Rest of members present helped prepare meat for noon and evening barbeques. Days were spent sleeping, hiking, horsebackriding, boating, swimming, and visiting. Feasts consisted of barbequed mutton, corn, coffee, and fried bread. Evening activity of squaw dancing was at beach, as recreation building was in use. Navajo singers came from as far away as Barstow. An excellent time was had by all."

Feb. 21, 1960. The show which is to be at the Shrine Auditorium during the second week of March, under which we as a club are entering an exhibit, was discussed. Mr. Allan Hill reported just about everything was ready except they will need dancers, weavers, sandpainters to perform. Mr. MacDonald appointed Mr. Gorman to chair the Navajo song group and to head the March 6 Indian program.

Oct. 5, 1962. Finance committee meeting. Carl Gorman introduced a motto for the Navajo Club, "It's not what the Navajo Club can do for you—but what you can do for the Club."

GLOSSARY

Anasazi. 'Anaasází—ancient people inhabiting Four Corners area (New Mexico, Arizona, Utah, Colorado). ('anaa—war, enemy, stranger + sází—ancestor). Usually translated "ancient enemies."

Atsidi-Sani. 'Atsidii—smith; sání—old; "old smith."

Bahajibah. Name as spelled in Alice Gorman's Bible. Bahajibaa', a female war name—"she started on a raid."

Barboncito. Chief spokesman for the Navajo at Fort Sumner (Bosque Redondo); Barboncito is a Spanish name.

Beshthlagai-ilth'ini Althts'osigi. Phonetic spelling. The spelling from the records of the Franciscan Fathers at St. Michael's, Arizona is: Besh-łagai ił'ini Ałts'osigi. Bééshłigaii—silver + 'ííł'íní—maker of it + 'ałts'óózí—slender +(í)gíí—the one that. "Slender maker of silver."

Bilagáana. Meaning "whiteman," from Spanish Americano.

Bilkijizbah. Carl's grandmother, Alice's mother. Name as spelled in Alice Gorman's Bible. Biłk'ídjizbah, a female war name—"intermingled in a raid."

Chahadin Benally. Navajo hataałii on Advisory Board of Navajo Culture Center, ONEO. Ch'ah—hat + 'ádin—nothing + binálí—paternal grandparent. "Grandson of No Hat."

Chinle. Chinle, Arizona, at the mouth of Canyon de Chelly. Ch'íníli—to flow out horizontally as a stream from a canyon.

Denetsosie. Navajo hataałii on Advisory Board of Navajo Culture Center, ONEO. Diné—man + ts'ósi—slender, "slender man."

Dibé thlizhiní. Dibé—sheep + łizhiní—black. The black sheep clan people.

Dibeh. Phonetic spelling for Navajo sheep, dibé.

Diné bikéyeh. Diné—man, person, Navajo; bi—his; keyah—land, country, nation. Navajo land.

Dineh. Phonetic spelling for diné—man, Navajo people.

Dzilth nát'oh. Dził—mountain + nát'oh—tobacco. A wild mountain tobacco.

Hataathlii. Hataałii: hataał—he sings + ii—the one, "Singer, chanter." Commonly translated "medicine man."

Jeddito. Jeddito, Arizona, in Navajo-Hopi disputed area. Jadi—antelope; to—water. Literally, antelope-water, meaning "where the antelope got their water."

Kaibeto. Kaibeto, Arizona. K'ai'—willow; bii'—in them; tó—water, spring. Literally, "spring in the willows."

Kee. Navajo name, spelled "Kii" when used as part of Navajo name with Navajo spelling; short for 'ashkii—boy.

K'i'dilyé. Planting (farming). A long time ago wedding ceremonies were called k'i'dilyé.

Kin-ya-onny beyeh. The signature Carl Gorman used on many paintings. Originally he used Ki-ya-onny beyeh, from kin-yaa'áanii—the Towering House People Clan, his father's clan. Biyé—his son: "Son to all the Towering House People."

Náneeskaadí. Tortilla. Náneeskaad—it was patted + -í—the one, referring to method of shaping. A thick flour tortilla.

Nazlini. Nazlini, Arizona. Názłíní means "it makes a turn flowing."

Peshlakai. Family spelling of the name today. It was "Beshłagai" in church records at St. Michael's Mission. Beeshłigaii—silver. Literally, beesh—metal; ligaii—it is white; +-ii—the one.

Sa'ą nagaí k'ad bik'eh hózhǫ. Final vowels in sa'á and hózhó are nazalized like saying, sa'on and hózhóhn. Literally, sá—old age; nagaí—walking; k'ad—now; bik'eh—according to; hózhǫ—to be in harmony. It is generally translated as some form of walking with long life according to a path of harmony or beauty. Hataałii do not (usually) give a clear meaning of this.

Shashjaa'. Bear's Ears, Utah (near Bluff City, Utah); a pair of promontories. (shash, bear + jaa', ear).

Shidiné'é. Shi—my + diné'é—people.

Shima yazzie. Maternal aunt. Shimá—my mother + yázhí—little. Literally, "little mother."

Táchii 'nii. The red running into water people clan.

Tkele-cho-gi. Phonetic spelling for jackass, téliichogii.

Tsah-as-zih. Phonetic spelling for Tsá'ászi, yucca.

Tselaa. Old Navajo name meaning "refuge" and referring to rock known today as Fortress Rock. "Fortress" is not a translation of its Navajo name. There is an old ruin on top. The area is known today as Tsé láni, "many rocks," Salina, Arizona.

Woll-a-chee. Phonetic spelling for red ant, wóláchíí.

Yá 'át 'ééh shidine 'é. Literally, yá 'át 'ééh—greetings; shi—my; dine'é—people, meaning "greetings my people."

Yei-bi-chei. Phonetic spelling for Yé'ii bicheii. Yé'ii—Holy One(s); bi—his + cheii—grandfather. Literally, "Holy One, his grandfather." Refers to masked dancers in the nine-night ceremony commonly called the Yé'ii bicheii.

Zonnie. A Navajo name usually so spelled; derived from words for "womenfolk"—sáanii—and "woman"—'asdzání, 'asdzą́ą́, 'asdzáán.

Note: ł, slashed l is pronounced thl when followed by a vowel, as: thla.
       It is pronounced lth when preceded by a vowel, as: ilth.
   ´ is an accent mark
   ' is a glottal stop
   ˛ ˛ marks under vowels means to nasalize the vowel, as: een

SELECTED BIBLIOGRAPHY

Beck, Peggy V., and A. L. Walters. *The Sacred: Ways of Knowledge, Sources of Life.* Tsaile, Ariz.: Navajo Community College, 1977.

Forbes, Jack D. *Apache, Navajo and Spaniard.* Norman: University of Oklahoma Press, 1960.

Gilpin, Laura. *The Enduring Navajo.* Austin: University of Texas Press, 1968.

Grant, Campbell. *Canyon del Chelly: Its People and Rock Art.* Tucson: University of Arizona Press, 1978.

Kahlenberg, Mary Hunt, and Anthony Berlant. *The Navajo Blanket.* New York: Praeger Publishers, 1972.

Kluckhohn, Clyde, and Dorothea Leighton. *The Navajo,* rev. ed. Garden City, N.Y.: Doubleday and Co., 1962.

Link, Martin A., ed. *Navajo. A Century of Progress 1868–1968.* Window Rock, Ariz.: Navajo Tribe, 1968.

McAllister, Davis P., ed., and Mary C. Wheelwright. *The Great Star Chant.* Santa Fe: Museum of Navajo Ceremonial Art, 1956.

McAllister, Davis P. *Hogans, Navajo Houses, and House Songs.* Middletown, Conn.: Wesleyan University Press, 1980.

Monthan, Doris. *R. C. Gorman: The Lithographs.* Flagstaff, Ariz.: Northland Press, 1978.

Newcomb, Franc Johnson. *Hosteen Klah.* Norman: University of Oklahoma Press, 1964.

Newcomb, Franc J., and Gladys Reichard. *Sand Paintings of the Navajo Shooting Chant.* New York: Dover Publications, 1975.

Ortiz, Alfonso, ed. *New Perspectives on the Pueblo.* Albuquerque: University of New Mexico Press, 1972.

Paul, Doris A. *Navajo Code Talkers.* Philadelphia: Dorrance and Co., 1973.

Pike, Donald G. *Anasazi: Ancient People of the Rock.* Palo Alto, Calif.: American West Publishing Co., 1974.

Reichard, Gladys A. *Navajo Religion: A Study of Symbolism.* Princeton, N.J.: Princeton University Press, 1974.

Roessel, Ruth, and Broderick H. Johnson. *Navajo Livestock Reduction: A National Disgrace.* Chinle, Ariz.: Navajo Community Press, 1974.

Roessel, Ruth. *Navajo Stories of the Long Walk Period.* Chinle, Ariz.: Navajo Community College Press, 1973.

Rodee, Marian E. *Old Navajo Rugs: Their Development from 1900 to 1940.* Albuquerque: University of New Mexico Press, 1981.

Sandner, Donald. *Navajo Symbols of Healing.* New York: Harcourt, Brace, Jovanovich, 1979.

Sando, Joe S. *The Pueblo Indians.* San Francisco: Indian Historian Press, 1976.

Woodward, Arthur. *Navajo Silver.* Flagstaff, Ariz.: Northland Press, 1971.

Young, Robert W., and William Morgan. *The Navajo Language: A Grammar and Colloquial Dictionary.* Albuquerque: University of New Mexico Press, 1980.

INDEX

Carl Gorman's World

Designed by Barbara Jellow
Composed by the University of New Mexico Printing Plant
in VIP Trump Medieval
Printed and bound by Malloy Lithographing, Inc.
Color sections and dust jacket
printed in Japan by DNP (America), Inc.